The Boomer Retirement Time Bomb

The Boomer Retirement Time Bomb

How Companies Can Avoid the Fallout from the Coming Skills Shortage

Donald L. Venneberg and
Barbara Welss Eversole

 PRAEGER

AN IMPRINT OF ABC-CLIO, LLC
Santa Barbara, California • Denver, Colorado • Oxford, England

Library of Congress Cataloging-in-Publication Data

Venneberg, Donald L.
    The boomer retirement time bomb : how companies can avoid the fallout from the coming skills shortage / Donald L. Venneberg and Barbara Welss Eversole.
        p. cm.
    Includes bibliographical references and index.
    ISBN 978-0-313-37538-5 (hard copy : alk. paper) — ISBN 978-0-313-37539-2 (ebook) 1. Baby boom generation—Employment—United States. 2. Older people—Employment—United States. 3. Baby boom generation—Retirement—United States. 4. Employees—Training of—United States. I. Eversole, Barbara Welss. II. Title.
    HD6280.V46   2010
    658.3—dc22   2010015823

ISBN: 978-0-313-37538-5
EISBN: 978-0-313-37539-2

14 13 12 11 10   1 2 3 4 5

This book is also available on the World Wide Web as an eBook.
Visit www.abc-clio.com for details.

Praeger
An Imprint of ABC-CLIO, LLC

ABC-CLIO, LLC
130 Cremona Drive, P.O. Box 1911
Santa Barbara, California 93116-1911

This book is printed on acid-free paper ∞

Manufactured in the United States of America

Contents

Acknowledgments

We could not have completed this book without the help of our colleagues, Stephanie Mace at Colorado State University, and Yi Chew and Cindy Crowder at Indiana State University. Their time and effort in assisting us with research, editing, and general constructive critiquing of our work as it progressed was invaluable. In addition, Barbara would like to thank her husband, Charles, and their two sons, Birch and Christopher, and Donald would like to thank his wife Gail for their patience and support throughout this project.

CHAPTER 1

Introduction

Everyone is the age of their heart.

Guatemalan Proverb

THE POPULATION IS GETTING OLDER AND SO IS THE WORKFORCE

Throughout human history, with some exceptions, most countries had more young people than old people. This is no longer true in the United States and is even less true in most Western European countries and Japan. Life expectancy in the United States has been steadily increasing and stood at almost seventy-eight years at the end of 2007 (just over seventy-five for men and eighty for women) (Xu, Kochanek and Tejada-Vera 2009). As former chairman of the Federal Reserve Peter Peterson stated in his 2004 book, *Running On Empty:*

> . . . between now and 2040 the number of "elderly" Americans (aged sixty-five and over–or so convention has it) will more than double while the nonelder population will grow by just 10 percent. Thirty-five years ago the future was crowded with babies. Today, it's crowded with seniors. (p. 56)

In a parallel to Peter Peterson's statement above, a 2004 article by Ken Dychtwald and others with the *Harvard Business Review* noted the impact of this change in the proportion of senior workers in the workforce:

> The proportion of workers over 55 declined from 18% in the 1970s to under 11% in 2000—but it's projected to rebound to 20% by 2015. . . . Just when we've gotten accustomed to having relatively few mature workers around, we have to start learning how to attract and retain far more of them. (Dychtwald, Erickson and Morison 2004, p. 49)

In the middle of the first decade of this century about 75 percent of men and 90 percent of women over age sixty-five were no longer in paid occupations (Atchley and Barusch 2004). Between 1977 and 2007, employment of workers sixty-five and over increased 101 percent, compared to a much smaller increase of 59 percent for total employment (age sixteen and over). The number of employed men sixty-five and over rose 75 percent, but employment of women sixty-five and older increased by nearly twice as much, climbing 147 percent. The number of employed people over age seventy-five was only 0.8 percent, but this group had the most dramatic gain, increasing 172 percent between 1977 and 2007. Although rare, it is becoming less unusual to find a few workers still active in the workforce at age one hundred. It should be noted that none of this increase includes the Baby Boomers. The leading edge of that cohort has not yet reached age sixty-five.

By 2016, workers age sixty-five and over are expected to account for 6.1 percent of the total labor force, up sharply from their 2006 share of 3.6 percent (Bureau of Labor Statistics 2008). By 2016, many of those over sixty-five who are workers will be Baby Boomers. They will become the largest and fastest growing segment in the U.S. workforce (Moseley and Dessinger 2007).

As of December 2009, workers from the 76-million-member cohort of Baby Boomers (born between 1946 and 1964) constituted 40.7 percent of the U.S. labor force over twenty years of age (Bureau of Labor Statistics 2009). The leading edge of these Boomer workers will begin to move into the traditional retirement age of sixty-five in 2011. The Boomers are followed by a much smaller Generation X cohort (some 51 million born between 1965 and 1979). Generation X workers are 34 percent of the workforce over age twenty. Workers from the following Generation Y or Millennial cohort (some 70 million born between 1980 and 1995) are 20.7 percent of the workforce over age twenty. The small remaining balance of workers are in the age group sixty-five and above.

THE WORKFORCE GAP

Sign, sign, everywhere a sign
. . . do this, don't do that, can't you read the sign.
Five Man Electrical Band (1970, 2002)

As the U.S. workforce ages, some analysts and researchers are projecting a labor shortage and a corresponding job boom in the next decade (Challenger 2003; Herman, Olivo and Gioia 2003; Penner, Perun and Steuerle 2002), especially for skilled and experienced workers (Schweyer 2003). The signs are pointing to a gap in the availability of an educated and trained pool of skilled workers to fill organizational needs by the end of this decade. The gap is in part caused by demography (Kaihla 2003), the U.S. philosophy and practice toward restricting immigration (Huber and Espenshade 1997), and current government, organizational, and social policies and practices that limit the retention and hiring of older workers (Atchley and Barusch 2004; Auerbach and Welsh 1994; Dychtwald 1999; Goldberg 2000; Penner, Perun and Steuerle 2002).

During the decade 2010–2020, the members of the Millennial generation will be moving into the workforce in greater numbers. However, it will be at least a decade or more beyond that before the Millennials represent a significant portion of those in the prime age workforce and begin to become leaders and managers. Also, in many cases it will take that long for them to gain the necessary skill and experience of Baby Boomer workers or the more senior Generation X workers. Prior to that point, most organizations will be competing mainly for the smaller numbers of Generation X workers to fill positions requiring skill and experience and for managerial and leadership positions vacated by Baby Boomers (Challenger 2003; Gordon 2005; Herman, Olivo and Gioia 2003).

This lack of replacement talent will be exacerbated by a slowing growth in the workforce in general. The Bureau of Labor Statistics in 2001 projected that the total U.S. civilian labor force growth is expected to slow from an annual rate of 1.1 percent between 1990 and 2000 to 0.7 percent through 2025. It is expected that the prime workforce age group (usually considered to be those ages 25–54) will be in short supply for the next decade or two until those from Generation X gain sufficient experience to fill some of the key managerial and leadership positions, and the Millennials become sufficiently skilled and developed to fill professional and technical jobs at the full performance level in organizations (Herman, Olivo and Gioia 2003). At the same time that the median age of American workers has been steadily increasing, the number of workers ages 25–39 has been decreasing. In this scenario, if all the baby boomers were to retire at traditional retirement age, then there wouldn't be enough workers to meet the needs of businesses. Finding qualified applicants to fill key positions becomes harder because of the drain of experienced personnel in the workforce.

The short-term solution, which accelerated in the late 1990s and into the first decade of this century, has been for organizations to move jobs offshore, with some consideration for keeping a few older workers longer, and to replace people with technology. By the period 2015–2020, these options may become less viable. At that point, organizations will need to be in position to support much higher levels of investment in training their senior workers and retaining more of them to make up for the shortfall of experienced workers from the small generation cohort (Gordon 2005).

RETAINING AND HIRING SENIOR WORKERS TO FILL THE GAP

This source of experienced, skilled, and knowledgeable senior workers could remain available to carry organizations through the gap. To be able to retain the senior workers that organizations have, however, they will need to reverse the current trend toward pushing these seasoned workers out of the job market through an enduring youth bias and retirement policies that incentivize early retirement. Also, organizations will need to consider proactively recruiting former workers who are seniors (either from their own organizations or from other organizations) to fill key positions with the experience, skills, and knowledge that only they possess. In addition, organizations will need to build on the strengths of and encourage teamwork among their intergenerational employees.

Some organizations are beginning to understand the dimensions of the problem, and are becoming concerned about the potential loss of knowledge and skills as senior workers approach retirement. However, many employers do not fully understand the issues surrounding the drivers for older workers staying in or leaving their organizations, and are thus still unprepared for these challenges. There are a number of countervailing forces impacting the decision of a senior worker to retire or stay in the workforce. For example, there appears to be an increasing desire by senior workers to continue to work longer, moderated by the availability of an age-friendly workplace and increased workplace flexibility, and a desire by senior workers for more work-life balance (see Chapter 4 for more details on workplace flexibility). This force is somewhat countered by the degree to which senior workers find an atmosphere of age discrimination or devaluation of their skills, knowledge, and abilities in the workplace.

Also, as with all age groups, burnout or illness can be a driver to leave the job. In addition, the growing shift by companies to defined benefit retirement plans based on self-directed investment by the employee and its concomitant increased risk (witness the substantial loss of value of retirement assets in these plans in the recent recession) has motivated senior workers to remain on the job.

Fortunately, senior workers increasingly want to work past traditional retirement age. The American Association of Retired People (AARP) reported in 2003 that 69 percent of employees over the age of forty-five are planning to work past the age of sixty-five (Roper Starch 1999). The attitude of senior workers toward retirement also seems to be changing. A study of Baby Boomer workers by AARP (Montenegro, Fischer and Remez 2002) confirmed that as many as 70 percent of Boomer workers want to continue to work and contribute past the "normal" retirement age. Another study found that the average age at retirement in the United States is now around sixty-four, but is expected to increase in the coming decades (Toossi 2004).

Older workers are also showing an increasing interest in remaining on the job in a full-time status. Since the mid-1990s there has been a dramatic shift in the part-time versus full-time status of older workforce. The ratio of part-time to full-time employment among older workers was relatively steady from 1977 through 1990. Between 1990 and 1995, part-time work among older workers began trending upward with a corresponding decline in full-time employment. But after 1995, that trend began a marked reversal with full-time employment rising sharply. Between 1995 and 2007, the number of older workers on full-time work schedules nearly doubled while the number working part-time rose just 19 percent. As a result, full-timers now account for a majority among older workers: 56 percent in 2007, up from 44 percent in 1995. This means that the drain on the workforce can be staved off while giving older people the chance to keep working and sharing their knowledge and training with younger employees.

THE BOOMER RETIREMENT TIME BOMB: THE TIMER HAS SLOWED, BUT NOT STOPPED

There is considerable controversy among public policy makers, business leaders, and others who study workforce issues over whether or not the large cohort of Baby Boomer workers who are in the workforce today will soon begin retiring in large numbers. Looking to past behavior of workers who have retired from the workforce is not much help in projecting the future behavior of the Baby Boomers, since the Boomers' attitudes toward work and retirement differ from those of past generations. For example, in 1996, 41 percent of Baby Boomers said they wanted to retire before age fifty-nine. However, of the prior generation, Veteran retirees, only 19 percent had actually retired by age fifty-nine in 1996 (Schanes 1996, as cited in Choo 1999). The data for the young retirees (before age 59) is limited, but a study by the national academy on an aging society (2000) estimated that approximately 10 percent of non-working men and women in the United States between the ages of 51 and 59 were retired. (See reference list.)

Of course the economic downturns and recession in the first decade of this century have had a dampening effect on retirement as potential retirees have lost a considerable amount of their assets in the value of their homes and their stock and mutual fund portfolios. This has caused most Boomers to rethink their retirement strategy and timing. However, when the economy turns around, the Boomers will likely feel freed of their economic restraints and head for the door. In a recent conversation with one of the authors, William Rothwell, who studies the aging workforce and the development of older workers, noted that in his opinion "as soon as the economy gets better, we are going to see a mass exodus of older workers . . . many will go overseas where their expertise is valued and where age is not seen as a detriment as it is here" (personal contact, November 2009).

THE GENDER MIX OF THE POPULATION AND THOSE OF PRIME WORKFORCE AGE

The number of women in the U.S. population has exceeded the number of men since 1950. Although this gap narrowed from 6.2 million to 5.3 million between 1990 and 2000, women continued to outnumber men in the population as a whole in 2000. In older age groups, the ratio of male to female in the U.S. population shifts toward a higher proportion of women. In 2000, the male-female ratio was 105 for the 15–24 age groups, but dropped to 92.4 for the 55–64 age groups. At the upper age range, women considerably outnumber men, with a male-female ratio of 40.7 for the group aged 85 and over. In the prime age workforce ages 25–54, within the total population, the male-female ratio reflected a larger number of women for all but the youngest age group, 25–34, where the ratio reflected slightly more men at 101.8. For the other two prime age workforce groups, the ratio favored women. For the age group 35–44, the male-female ratio was 98.9 and for the age group 45–54, the ratio was 96.4

(Smith and Spraggins 2001). In addition, women are becoming the larger portion of the educated class in the United States. Over half of all college students, and in particular graduate students, in U.S. colleges and universities are women.

For most of the twentieth century, women were particularly disadvantaged in preparing for retirement due to their usually lower pay or their dependency on the assets and retirement benefits of their spouses, as well as social expectation of women as caregivers for both children and the elderly (Calasanti and Slevin 2001). While this gender gap, at least for pay, has been shrinking, it still exists.

However, in terms of outlook toward retirement, there appear to be decreasing gender differences in the outlook of senior workers on whether or not they will continue to work either for the same company or for another company in retirement. Results from a Retirement Confidence Survey by the Employee Benefits Research Institute (2004) reflect that currently employed women and men are about equal in their level of confidence that they will have adequate income and assets in retirement to support a comfortable lifestyle. Of course, these 2004 studies were conducted before the current economic recession.

In any case, it is to be expected that both men and women will desire, and will be increasingly able (or financially compelled), to work past the traditional retirement age of sixty-five. This trend to working longer should be good news for society as a whole and taxpayers in particular, considering that the ratio of workers to pensioners in the United States is currently slightly less than four to one and declining (Bongaarts 2004). This trend, if it continues, should also be positive for businesses and other organizations because it gives them a bit of breathing room to plan for the upcoming large brain drain when the Boomer retirement time bomb does eventually go off. However, there is a danger in this present era of high unemployment and downsizing by companies that business leaders will become complacent about the need for retaining and effectively using the talent they have residing in their senior workers. We believe that this complacency will cause headaches for most organizations that require a highly talented workforce to maintain competitive advantage. Despite the current situation, the Boomers will eventually leave the full-time active workforce, taking all their knowledge and experience with them.

TREATING SENIOR WORKERS AS VALUED ASSETS AND KEEPING THEM ENGAGED

To help overcome these limitations, organizational leaders will need to design and implement policies, processes, and workplace changes to better accommodate and leverage the valuable asset resident in their senior skilled and experienced workers if they are to retain the asset and use it effectively to meet organizational objectives. The shortfall of skilled workers resulting from this demographic shift should also motivate organizations to retain and recruit senior workers and retirees to fill the gap. These issues will be further discussed in Chapters 2 and 3.

RETIRED AND DISPLACED SENIOR WORKERS AS EMPLOYEES TO FILL CRITICAL TALENT SHORTAGES

While not all senior workers have the talent and skills (current or potential) to fill the needs of organizations, neither do all younger workers. The key for organizational leaders is to equally consider the knowledge, skills, and abilities that potential employees from all age groups bring to the table and fully recognize the special, often tacit, abilities that experienced senior workers might add to an organization's workforce when recruiting to fill key positions. We discuss this area further in Chapter 4.

THE INCREASING DEMAND FOR WORK-LIFE BALANCE

As the workforce becomes both older and increasingly multigenerational, organizations will progressively need to consider both the different and similar needs of members of generational cohorts for flexibility in the work environment. Organizations will also have to continually adapt their workplace policies and practices, including their recruiting, retention, training, and career development policies and processes, to accommodate this intergenerational mix. One particular issue that will need to be addressed is handling the supervisor-supervisee relationship when the supervisee is much older than the supervisor. Responsibility and authority in organizations that used to be synonymous with seniority and age will be owned increasingly by younger generation workers. We discuss the work-life balance and provide suggestions for workplace accommodation in Chapter 5.

MANAGING THE INTERGENERATIONAL WORKFORCE

In 2010, it is expected that most of the U.S. workforce will consist of members of three generational cohorts: the Baby Boomers, Generation X, and the Millennials. In addition, there will likely still be a few workforce members from the Veterans generation. The mix of the overall U.S. workforce in 2010 will be concentrated in young workers (18–25) and senior workers (55 and above), with a much smaller (26–54) age group in the middle (Lerman and Schmidt 2002). Within these generational cohorts, individuals are diverse and have unique sets of values, skills, and knowledge. However, they do share many common value sets that impact their method of working in and their desires from the workplace. The challenges for making effective use of the varied strengths that the generations bring (and the potential conflicts) will need to be accommodated in training, developing, and motivating the multigenerational work teams in organizations. We discuss the challenge and opportunity offered by the intergenerational workforce in Chapter 6.

THE NEW VIEW OF RETIREMENT: PARTIAL AND CYCLICAL VERSUS TERMINAL

For most of the last half of the twentieth century, retirement was viewed as a natural progression in one's life (following early development, education, and a work career). Things began to shift, however, late in the century, and today the concept of *retirement* is moving toward an idea of some form of continued work engagement either in one's current field or profession or toward an entirely new field or endeavor. Also, the processes of bridge employment or a gradual tapering off from full-time employment, continuing work for an organization in a part- or full-time consulting role, and other alternatives to the terminal form of retirement are increasingly coming to the fore. We discuss these areas further in Chapter 7.

IMPLICATIONS FOR ORGANIZATIONS

Given these shifts in demography and in employee needs (or demands) it will be incumbent on the leaders of businesses in the future to adjust their talent recruiting and retention systems and adjust their workplaces and human resource policies and practices to accommodate both senior and younger workers with diverse needs in the intergenerational workforce. The organizations that are most successful in providing an organizational climate where all generations can work together will be able to attract and retain the most talented workers.

The purpose of this book is to shed some light on the issues around retaining, and even recruiting, talent from the pool of senior experienced workers to smooth the transition from the upcoming retirement of workers from the Boomer generation. We also will provide some suggested considerations for workplace policies and practices to accommodate the diverse needs of both senior and younger workers and to best manage an intergenerational workforce.

CHAPTER 2

Are Senior Workers an Asset or a Liability?

The years teach much which the days never knew.
Ralph Waldo Emerson (1803–1882)

THE VALUE OF OLDER WORKERS: EDUCATION, SKILL, LOYALTY, AND RELIABILITY

Older workers have intrinsic assets which can be brought to bear on solving organizational problems, mentoring younger workers, and providing insight born of experience to everyday business practices. Not utilizing these assets is akin to leaving money on the table. Ken Dychtwald and his associates (2006) note that workers over age fifty-five hold college undergraduate degrees in about the same proportion (35 percent) as younger cohorts, but they have the highest incidence of graduate degrees. Workers over fifty-five have high overall satisfaction rates with their jobs (68 percent) and their managers (54 percent).

The Baby Boomer portion of those workers over age fifty-five has also generally attained higher levels of education than their predecessor generational cohorts. Additionally, they have developed values and attitudes favorable to continued work and may wish to remain active in the workforce longer than their predecessors, absenting health and other issues limiting their abilities (Besl and Kale 1996). Some other recent studies have also shown that some employers are recognizing other strengths that senior employees bring to issues of productivity and goal accomplishment, such as a strong work ethic, reliability, and high levels of skill (James, Swanberg and McKechnie 2007).

These generalizations do not apply across the board, of course. Not all Baby Boomers are well educated and have access to resources to keep their skills up to date in a competitive job market. Some early Baby Boomers now in their sixties have lower skill levels and face poverty or marginal income levels that may prevent them from retiring or finding work sufficient to support them. Many lower-educated and single older women are at a particular disadvantage in this regard (Taylor and Geldhauser 2007). In addition, not all senior workers have a stronger work ethic or loyalty to the organization and its mission and goals than their younger counterparts.

Juhani Ilmarinen (2003) created a model based on his Work Ability index to reflect the factors which enable or prevent a person from being an effective worker when older. The ground level support for Work Ability is *health and functional capacities*, which incorporates physical, mental, and social dimensions with the health of the worker. The next level represents the *competence* of the worker, which includes his or her knowledge, skills, and need for lifelong learning. The third level is made up of *values, attitudes, and motivations* of the worker. The fourth level describes the *work* itself, which includes the dimensions of the *community* and *environment* and the exposure to the *demands* of the work. Management is also a key characteristic of this level, as managers have the authority and responsibility to modify the dimensions of work, such as providing physical accommodation and flexible work schedules for older workers.

INCREASED COST VERSUS INCREASED VALUE OF SENIOR WORKERS

Steven Stern is one of the early proponents of considering the labor market economics of the relationship of ability of workers relative to the age of retirement as driven by organizational considerations. In a 1994 study, he found that when making decisions on retention of senior workers, organizations take a liability perspective instead of an asset perspective. Thus, organizations focus on the increased cost of senior workers, in terms of salary and benefits, without considering the level of ability of senior workers in relation to younger workers.

Taking this liability or cost approach has led many organizations to provide incentives for senior workers to retire early. This was probably a rational choice, at least partially, in the 1970s and early 1980s in order to provide jobs and incentives for the large number of younger

Baby Boomers who were entering the workforce and moving up organizational ladders. It also made sense for organizations that needed to downsize in reaction to economic downturns to shed some of their senior workers in a humane and orderly fashion.

The main factor influencing this decision by organizations to shed senior workers is that senior workers are often paid more. It is also believed that senior workers can be easily replaced by less experienced but lower-paid younger workers. Unfortunately, this again is a cost calculation without regard to the value of the additional experience and knowledge possessed by senior workers. Some more enlightened organizations have now found that much of the knowledge and experience of senior workers cannot be easily replaced in the short term.

Managers also often assume that senior workers are more rigid in their response to change. However, in studies where older and younger workers were involved in a change process in organizations, there were no discernable differences in their positive or negative response to change based on their age (Hedge, Borman and Lammlein 2006).

While it is true that older persons, in general, are more subject to illness as they age, and thus use more health benefits provided by organizations, this is not a truism for all people. Lifestyle factors, genetics, and the environment of the workplace itself can contribute to, or work against, an increase in illness and the use of health benefits due to aging.

One of the ways to ease the loss of talent in retiring employees is to offer them some sort of transitional or bridge employment or retirement option in lieu of laying them off or encouraging them to retire altogether. We discuss bridge employment and retirement in more detail in Chapters 5 and 7.

BEYOND AGE DISCRIMINATION: SHIFTING ORGANIZATIONAL CULTURE AND VIEWS ON SENIOR WORKERS

In the United States, we hold a divided view of aging. On one hand, we are concerned with the negative aspects of aging, such as declining health, limited mobility, reduced access to services, and disconnection from family and friends. This fosters the concepts that people should "grow old gracefully" and "act their age." On the other hand, especially as the Baby Boomers are aging and becoming more prevalent in the national consciousness, we increasingly talk of "productive aging" (Schulz 2001) or "successful aging" (McHugh 2003) in terms of better health, more recreation, and increased time flexibility to pursue personal interests and education. We are also seeing a growing view that the traditional retirement-to-old-age phase of life is now shifting to a *third age* in which

. . . the workspace becomes a dynamic space for older workers, [work] . . . becomes a search for continued meaning and contribution as well as to satisfy a financial need, [and] . . . older workers might make the decision to remain in, retire from or return to periods of part-time, full-time or seasonal or holiday work. (Rocco, Stein and Lee 2003, p. 156)

Older persons were once revered for their wisdom and knowledge in the United States, as they still are in some agricultural and subsistence societies. However, older persons have become increasingly marginalized as being old, frail, unattractive, and nonproductive in the United States. Many U.S. companies do not consider older persons as a primary source of workers.

The American Association of Retired Persons (AARP) has conducted periodic surveys since 1985 of senior level human resource executives in organizations of over fifty employees on the subject of perceptions of older workers. These surveys were administered in 1985, 1989, 1994 and 1998. The results of the surveys show remarkable consistency over the fourteen-year period. The common findings from the studies reveal that employers rate older workers highly on loyalty, dependability, experience, and customer relations. However, they rate older workers less favorably on flexibility, adaptability, technological competence, and ability to learn new technology (Rix 2001).

In recent years, some interest has been demonstrated by a limited number of companies for retaining or regaining the potential human and social capital resident in the growing cohort of senior workers. A lesser effort has been made by companies to actively seek and recruit retirees. One notable example is the effort by Home Depot, in concert with AARP, to recruit retirees with specific skills into their stores. However, senior workers' training and development needs, workplace and work schedule concerns, and work aspirations are often not fully understood or considered when designing and implementing workforce policies and practices that impact senior workers' decisions to stay in, leave, or return to the workforce.

In addition, there is an enduring built-in bias to a youth-oriented culture and outright age discrimination in some organizations in hiring, promotion, and layoffs or firing (Johnson and Neumark 1997; Seagrave 2001). The impact of this youth culture is that senior workers are often devalued in the workplace and thus subtly or overtly encouraged to leave in order to make way for younger workers. The irony is that while workers are living longer, more productive lives, discrimination begins as young as age forty. When someone over forty loses their job, it is an upward battle to find a new position. Their experience is simply not valued as much as the newer and more organizationally and professionally relevant skills that younger people are assumed to have. It is easy to fall into the trap of assuming that age automatically determines relevant skills.

Various laws and regulations in the United States, beginning with the Age Discrimination in Employment Act (ADEA) of 1968, and the resultant lawsuits and rulings by the Equal Employment Opportunity Commission have ameliorated much of the overt age bias in organizations for hiring, promotion, and retention. Also, laws such as the ADEA and organizations such as AARP that lobby for equal consideration in employment and benefits for older Americans, seem to support our social norm of equity and reduction of prejudice. However, despite legal prohibitions, evidence of the continued existence of age bias can still be found in actual behavior by executives, managers, and human resources staffs in organizations (Seagrave 2001). Organizations tend to have youth-oriented cultures that are difficult to change, despite the existing antidiscrimination laws. Moreover, managers still tend to prefer subordinates who are younger than they are. Managers may be threatened by senior workers reporting to them.

SENIOR WORKERS DO NOT DECLINE IN VALUE TO THE ORGANIZATION, BUT THEIR VALUE MAY SHIFT

Most organizations are not considering the value added or the value shift which may accrue to senior workers in the organization. These value-added benefits come from senior workers' attitudes, behavior, knowledge, skills, abilities, and mentoring capacity as they move through the organization over time. This added value can and should be considered an asset to organizations and measured in terms of human capital and psychological and social capital.

Attitudes and Behavior

In today's work environment, organizations need to engage all employees to use their knowledge, skills, and abilities toward innovation and goal attainment. We support the claim by Nancy Ahlrichs (2007) that the observed attitude and behavior of older long-time employees as disengaged and "cruising to retirement" is actually a self-fulfilling prophecy fostered by organizations and their managers:

> Longtime employees who are told "just do your job. We'll ask if we want your ideas" follow those orders or leave. They have disengaged,

but they get up every day . . . they show up on time, but they leave their brain at the door. Salaried or hourly, too many just do their job, no more no less. (p. 4)

Organizations and managers who take this approach are "leaving money on the table" by disengaging a significant portion of their workers who have the potential to be excellent contributors. Boomers and their older colleagues (Veterans) would like to be sought out for advice, trained in the latest skills, and assigned to work on high-profile projects. They would like to be treated as up-and-comers just like their younger colleagues. If they are, they will give as much as any other employee. In addition, on average, Boomers and Veterans stay with the organization longer (ten years) versus their younger Generation X and Millennial colleagues (three years), providing a backbone of stability needed by most organizations.

Knowledge, Skills, and Abilities

There seems to be a belief among some managers and leaders that senior workers are lacking in needed technical skills and abilities. The reality, however, does not support this belief. For example, a study by Steven Allen (2001) found that contrary to the notion that technological change harms senior workers, the wage growth of experienced workers was much greater in industries with high research and development activity than those with little research and development activity.

Not all senior workers or all more junior workers have the abilities, attitudes, and work habits desired for long-term retention by organizations. However, the unique value of those senior workers with needed knowledge, skills, experience, and ability should be considered by organizations before deciding to offer or encourage early retirement.

From Individual Contributor to Mentor

As people move into midlife, what is important to them shifts. These shifts often result in angst and reevaluation of their priorities. Most often we hear of this in a negative form sometimes called the midlife crisis. In a more positive sense, midlife provides an opportunity to shift one's focus to higher-order concerns from personal achievement or success. In terms of career and work, these two domains have been conceptualized under the terms *agency* and *communion* (Calo 2007). Agency refers to one's primary motivation, achievement, mastery, power, and autonomy, all skills and abilities usually valued for success and moving up the ladder in an organization. Communion, on the other hand, refers to a primary motivation for intimacy, union with others, and openness. Agency thus reflects one's focus on self, whereas communion connotes a focus on others. Another term for this shift is the move by people in midlife to a stage called *generativity* (Erikson 1950, Jacques 1965 and Levinson 1978 as cited in Calo 2007) wherein ". . . humans have a strong need to expand ego interests beyond the self and to become a guider or contributor to succeeding generations" (Calo 2007, p. 388).

The value shift to communion and reaching the generativity stage provides a motivation for midlife workers to become mentors and pass on their knowledge and experience and assist junior members of organizations to grow and succeed. We discuss the role of mentoring in more detail in Chapter 3. As we also discuss in more detail in Chapter 5, the Millennial generation in particular will require mentoring and a high degree of supervision upon entering the workforce.

The Capital Value of Senior Workers

For both older and younger workers, their relationship with their organizations is increasingly temporary and transient. Leaders and managers of these organizations foster this view to a large degree by their behaviors toward their employees. Since the 1980s, and to a greater degree in the recessionary times during the first decade of the twenty-first century, employers have treated workers as interchangeable parts in the organization machine. They are a commodity to be used to accomplish goals and objectives and maximize profits much like other capital (e.g., buildings and machinery), and then to be disposed of when they are no longer needed. Taking this short-term economic view further, organizations often limit their investment in the human capital of their employees to that which is specific to the organization (e.g., skills and knowledge which can be used only or mostly within the organization). In fact, the prevailing view in organizations is that investments in more general skills and knowledge (such as general education, management skills, and interpersonal skills) that can be transferred by the employee to another organization or field are to be avoided.

The left-out element in this view is that of employee commitment. Employee commitment is the key element of a *psychological contract* between the employer and the employee. These contracts can be, and as noted above often are, *transactional* (fixed in scope and perhaps duration). Alternatively, organizations and employees can enter into a *relational* psychological contract wherein there are social and emotional exchanges; open-ended, longer-duration ties; and greater flexibility (Galunic and

Anderson 2000). It is this latter type of contract which more closely binds the employee to the organization and fosters organizational loyalty and continued personal commitment to organizational mission, goals, and objectives.

Human Capital, Social Capital, and Psychological Capital

There is little doubt that flawed perceptions of the value of older workers exist and serve as barriers in organizations. These barriers prevent organizations from realizing the contributions and value that older workers offer. We suggest that instead of a negative view toward older workers, organizations need to employ a positive perspective that recognizes the accumulated psychological, intellectual, emotional, and social capital that older workers possess, and in turn offer their employers. When deciding on the amount and type of investment in senior workers, it is helpful for managers and leaders to consider these workers in terms of the capital they represent to the company. The human, social, and psychological or emotional capital resident in a company's workers should be considered as a portfolio of assets that are used or available for both current and possible future needs. The unused capacity can be developed to meet company ends.

The *human capital* of workers is usually measured as the totality of their work skills and experience, and their education and training (Becker 1993). What is often not considered, however, is the more difficult-to-measure store of *social capital*, or unused capacity that workers have accumulated, that can add to or substitute for human capital. This capacity represents a passive or reserve capability and can become active in application to job and task performance (e.g., when a senior worker uses his or her informal networks with customers or other workers to facilitate getting things done outside normal channels). Senior workers generally have a large store of social capital, represented by their broad networks of social relationships with both those outside the organization and those within the organization. These relationships, which could be leveraged by organizations for the furtherance of organization ends, are often undervalued or overlooked altogether. This lack of regard by organizations for their existing human and social capital is viewed by Dess and Shaw (2001) as the primary determinant of productivity loss with the departure of older workers:

> . . . existing approaches estimate the effect of the departure of a long-tenured individual on organizational performance by (1) comparing the human capital accumulations of the departing employee

with the replacement and estimating the corresponding short-term productivity loss and/or (2) by estimating the short-term savings (e.g., lower pay) of the new employee versus replacement Although valuable, the approaches neglect to consider the value of the departing individual's social capital, his or her placement in the key social networks, and the corresponding and possibly long-term disruptions in these systems. (p. 450)

The concept of the interaction between an organization's human capital and social capital resident in its workers can be considered as a portfolio of assets that are currently used or available for possible future use. Simply put, senior workers know how to get things done through other people and have greater networks for getting resources. This social capital capacity often substitutes for additional human capital gained from formal training and education. However, this underlying capacity is not reflected in most company data on either the level or rate of participation or engagement in accomplishing goals and objectives (Fine and Green 2000), nor do most organizations have a method for measuring or evaluating this unused capacity (Geroy and Venneberg 2003).

Social capital has generally been recognized as actual and potential resources available and derived from relationships and networks of people. Invariably, older workers posses a greater degree of social capital. They have gained this capital because they have typically met more people and been involved in more social environments over the years than have younger workers. As well, they are more socialized in organizational culture, have a decreased learning curve, have acquired connections and relationships via the various networks and associations they have been a part of, and have experienced a broad range of interpersonal behaviors and relationships.

Having a workforce that knows where to find information and knows who in the organization or outside the organization has the necessary resources and abilities to get something done may be the most important asset an organization has. This networking ability is lost when the senior workers leave, as their relationships and networks go with them. It takes years for newly hired employees to develop such networks on their own.

A positive psychology approach to older workers can benefit any organization if managers and leaders focus on leveraging the strengths and talents of older workers in order to optimize organizational success (Peterson and Spiker 2005). Inaccurate and negative perceptions of older workers inhibit organizations from fully utilizing and capturing the positive contributions and economic value of employees in their middle and late career phases (Peterson and Spiker 2005). By embracing a positive psychological view, organizations will be more apt and able to implement programs to encourage the retention and further development of the Boomer generation. This cohort of older workers must be appreciated for the valuable human capital they embody, and organizations should aim to create human resource options that cater to the needs of these employees (Callanan and Greenhaus 2008).

According to Peterson and Spiker (2005), the positive psychology approach dictates that due to their greater overall human capital, denoted as the sum of psychological, intellectual, emotional, and social capital, older employees may contribute equal if not more value than younger employees. Two common myths perpetuate a negative view of older workers that the positive psychology perspective discounts based on previous research. The first myth is that older workers are not top learners. The second myth is that older workers are not top performers. In response to the first myth, a nationwide survey of 774 human resource directors conducted by Harris Interactive in 1999 revealed that 80 percent have less turnover; 75 percent have higher levels of commitment; 74 percent are more reliable; 71 percent have as much ability to acquire new skills; 62 percent are more creative and innovative; 80 percent have less absenteeism; 48 percent are more flexible and adaptable; and 49 percent are more motivated. As a result of this study, the Committee for Economic Development concluded that expanding the work-participation rate of older workers would enhance the learning and productivity of the workforce. With respect to the second myth, data have demonstrated that no significant difference in job performance exists between older and younger employees, and in reality, often older workers display slightly higher job performance than do younger workers (Peterson and Spiker 2005).

Intellectual capital consists of experience, skills, knowledge, intuition, and attitudes that have been cultivated over one's lifetime. Peterson and Spiker (2005) postulate that often, older workers have more of these abilities than do younger workers. Older workers, simply stated, have been involved and participating in the workforce for much longer than younger ones, and therefore, have accumulated more intellectual capital through years of experience. Replacing this cumulative knowledge and know-how that comes from time spent working is difficult to do.

Emotional capital contains the attributes of maturity, motivation, social skills, and self-regulation. According to developmental psychologists and gerontologists, self-awareness and self-exploration increase with age. Thus, older workers automatically have an advantage over younger workers due to age alone. As we grow older, we mature and develop.

In sum, it is difficult to replace the acquired confidence, emotional maturity, network or relationships, and years of experience that an older employee brings to the table. An older worker has valuable human capital that has accumulated over time, is not easily replaced, and likely is impossible to duplicate. The organizational outcomes of all four of these combined components of human capital lead to increased loyalty, decreased turnover, increased productivity, and the creation and retention of institutional memory (Peterson and Spiker 2005).

As we continue to move in the direction of the knowledge-based economy, older workers, with their added experience and acumen, are ideally suited to bring enhanced contributory value to organizations. Workers in this knowledge economy now constitute roughly two-thirds of the labor force. Employers should be warned that turning away older workers is a waste of human, social, intellectual, psychological, and emotional capital. A new perspective on what older members of society can bring to the workplace is much needed. Older workers have knowledge and wisdom from their many years in the field and overall combined life and work experiences (Knowledge@Wharton 2005). The Baby Boom generation comprises a pool of highly educated, talented, and experienced workers, who hold key leadership and management positions, and as such represent a critical resource that must be nurtured and maintained in order for organizations to continue to be successful (Callanan and Greenhaus 2008).

Senior Workers and Their Capability as Infrastructure

Another way to look at the unused capacity of senior workers could be as *infrastructure*. Companies could use this infrastructure of senior employees' knowledge of customers' needs and preferences gained over time for building and maintaining customer relationships. Internally, senior workers' knowledge of how things work could be used to transfer vital know-how to new employees to enhance organizational success. If all senior workers retire without transferring their infrastructure knowledge, the organization could face a huge loss in terms of organizational memory and learning. We have provided a suggested template at the end of this chapter to help managers, human resources managers, and leaders organize and value the assets resident in their senior workers.

Training and Development

Managers also often fail to invest in senior workers' training and development for future capacity at the same rate as they do for younger workers. Part of the reason for this lack of investment is that managers often believe senior workers lack interest in further training and

development. This is largely because of the belief that senior workers will not be with the organization much longer or the belief that they have reached their level of capability, resulting in what Ken Dychtwald (1999) calls a "silver ceiling" that stops upward mobility in the organization. There also seems to be a belief by some managers that senior workers do not want to be trained further. Contrary to these beliefs, a study by Patricia Simpson and her colleagues (2002) found that senior workers were more likely than younger workers to invest in developing *focused* skills that were *job-related*. In particular, those in the late career category, aged 50–65, were 1.5 to 2 times more likely than younger workers to invest in academic credentialing programs, targeted career- and job-related courses, and on-the-job based computer training.

The lack of continued investment in senior workers is also a result of beliefs and myths held by managers in organizations that senior workers become less flexible and lack the ability to learn and/or adapt to change as they age (Costello 1997; Goldberg 2000). Also, at least in the case of workers engaged in the more physical tasks in manufacturing and construction, they are more subject to accidents (Finley and Bennett 2002). Fortunately, research and the experience of managers and human resource professionals in practice have been emerging in recent years that are beginning to refute these myths (Goldberg 2000). For example, in a previous article, one of the authors and a colleague (Geroy and Venneberg 2003) noted that the value of individualism varied by generational cohort, which affected the strength of the preference by workers from these generational cohorts for the accumulation and use of both active and passive capacity in terms of skills and knowledge through education and training. Senior workers from the Boomer cohort are beginning to prefer more stability than individualism in their work lives. They are therefore more prone to accept the organization's desire to build active capacity for accomplishing existing or new tasks related to their current job. Unlike the Generation X and Millennial workers, the Baby Boomers are also less prone to push for opportunities to develop passive capacity to use for moving to other companies. Organizations would benefit from continuing to engage the Boomer generation of workers and extend the stability they offer to the workplace.

CAPTURING THE KNOWLEDGE, SKILLS, AND ABILITIES OF THE SENIOR WORKER

Most human resource managers in organizations have developed some methods and processes for inventorying the knowledge, skills, and abilities of their employees. These processes and methods often are called *knowledge management*. Knowledge management can take various forms, from keeping up-to-date information in employee personnel folders to more sophisticated databases, accessible by query or standard reports. A simple human capital assets matrix can sometimes suffice (see example under resources at the end of this chapter).

Whatever systems are used, they need to be systematically used for applying relevant knowledge, skills, and abilities (KSAs) to particular tasks or projects, or in forming effective teams. In particular, as noted above, the KSAs of senior workers need to be captured, especially those assets that are hard to measure such as tacit knowledge. It is not the purpose of this book to provide detailed human resource practices and processes to capture and use the KSAs of workers, as these methods are available from a variety of sources (see the resources section at the end of this chapter). Suffice it to say that when using any system and conducting any effort to increase employee engagement or to develop a talent management strategy for an organization, managers need to be sure that they also push for reigniting the engagement and productivity of longtime employees.

CONCLUSION

Senior workers represent a store of capacity in terms of knowledge and experience, and organizations should continue to value them and invest in their continued development. In order to turn away from the usual view of senior workers as a liability and an increasing cost, organizations need to rethink how they value the asset represented by senior workers. This shift will require redirection by leaders to change the workplace and the culture of their organizations to value and effectively use this asset. The following chapters provide additional insight and suggestions to accomplish this shift.

RESOURCES

General Human Resource Management and Training and Development

Society for Human Resource Management: www.shrm.org
American Society for Training and Development: www.astd.org

Guidance on Knowledge Management

Davenport, Thomas H. 2005. *Thinking for a living: How to get better performance and results from knowledge workers.* Cambridge, MA: Harvard Business School Press.

Stewart, Thomas A. 1997. *Intellectual capital: The new wealth of organizations.* New York: Doubleday.

————. 2001. *The wealth of knowledge: Intellectual capital and the twenty-first century organization.* New York: Doubleday.

Table 2.1
Human and Social Capital Assets Matrix

Employees by type and level	Years of formal education by field	Years of experience and area	Tacit knowledge & experience multiplier	Assessed value
Management				
Finance dept.				
Simpson, H.	18 (MBA)	10	1.4	39.2
Boop, B.	12 (BSBA)	6	1.2	21.6
Smith, S.	9 (BA, English)	12	1.0	21.0
Total	39	28		81.8

CHAPTER 3

Keeping Senior Workers as Engaged and Contributing Employees

Do not go gentle into that good night,
. . . rage, rage against the dying of the light.

Dylan Thomas (1914–1953)

SENIOR WORKERS' NEEDS FROM THE WORKPLACE

Senior workers' needs from the workplace may differ somewhat from those of workers in younger cohorts, but many of their needs (such as the need for work-life balance) are similar. Where they differ, in areas such as job satisfaction, the differences are often a matter of degree.

Engagement in Work in Later Life

Some research on attitudes toward work has suggested that more senior workers have higher levels of job satisfaction and positive attitudes. However, other studies have not completely confirmed this as a universally held attitude by all senior workers. More recently, it has been found that those senior workers who were more satisfied with their jobs were also those with higher pay and benefits than those with lower pay and benefits (Riordan, Griffith and Weatherly 2003 as cited in Barnes-Farrell and Matthews 2007). However, it has also been found that the strongest positive relationships between work and age are with the more intrinsic aspects of work, or the meaningfulness of work, than with pay and benefits (Barnes-Farrell and Matthews 2007). Of more interest to managers and leaders in organizations is that the level of satisfaction with one's job seems to follow a U-shaped course, with satisfaction declining until the worker reaches his or her mid-thirties and then generally increasing steadily until he or she reaches about age sixty. In a recent study of over 6,000 employees ages 18–94 in a large retail chain in the United States, it was found that those workers over age fifty-five were significantly more engaged than those under age fifty-four (James, Swanberg and McKechnie 2007). In the study findings, the authors noted that supervisor effectiveness was the key factor in the strength of employee engagement for older workers. This finding was consistent with that of similar studies for younger workers as well. The key element that a surveyed employee felt was important to their evaluation of supervisory effectiveness was the degree to which the supervisor provided them flexibility to take care of unexpected personal or family matters. They also cited having flexible work arrangements and, in particular, input to the choice of work schedules as a key component of their satisfaction with supervisors and their resulting feeling of engagement with the work and the organization.

In both research and practice, human resource professionals and managers of business units have often found that senior workers begin to shift their focus on what they want from training and other forms of knowledge acquisition, career development, challenging assignments, and the workplace in general (Lambrechts and Martens 2008). In a 2007 article, Diane Piktialis noted "older workers want the respect of other generations and they want to be valued by their managers and supervisors" and ". . . they want work arrangements that are flexible and benefits that are relevant to their life stage" (p. 79). Contrary to the belief held by a number of managers and some of their coworkers, senior workers are not usually "checking out" and cruising toward retirement in the latter part of their careers. Unfortunately, though, these attitudes lead to a perception by older workers that they are no longer valued, and are overlooked for development, promotion, and challenging work assignments.

Nonfinancial Reasons for Staying in the Workforce

A study by Montenegro, Fisher, and Remez (2002) found that there were increasingly nonfinancial reasons cited by those in the 50–70 age range for not retiring, such as a "desire to work for enjoyment," to "have something interesting to do," and "to stay physically active."

The study also suggested some elements of an organization and its workplace that may encourage senior workers to remain in the workforce:

1. The ability to continue to perform meaningful work where they can contribute their skill and knowledge
2. The availability of flexible work arrangements to meet family demands and to provide more leisure time
3. A workplace which accommodates their physical limitations, if necessary
4. An organization which continues to invest in developing new knowledge and skills
5. An ability to contribute to societal goals

Another study by Stein, Rocco, and Goldenetz (2000) found similar organizational elements and personal issues that may influence senior workers to remain in, retire from, or return to the workforce, in relation to training and development, career development, and organizational development policies and practices. Additionally, William Rothwell and his colleagues (2008) found from a study of older workers and their employers in Alabama that:

> The most attractive approaches the employers used to retain older workers were in providing opportunities for flexible work schedules, rehiring retirees as consultants, providing professional development opportunities, and offering part-time work with benefits. (p. 38)

A related factor for senior workers staying in their organizations is that they have often developed strong linkage to their careers. This is called by various names, but most commonly conceived of as *job embeddedness*. In a sense, job embeddedness is an entangling web in which the individual can get stuck to the job and career. The elements that reinforce this embeddedness are (1) the extent of the links the worker has to people and/or activities in the organization, (2) the extent to which their jobs and communities fit with other aspects of their lives, and (3) the sacrifices they would have to make to break these links (Mitchell, Holtmon, Lee, Sablynski and Erez 2001 as cited in Feldman 2007). In addition, those whose jobs are challenging and varied and not overly physically or emotionally stressful tend to stay in the workforce longer (Rothwell, Sterns, Spokus and Reaser 2008).

Job embeddedness can be reinforced and nurtured by organizations to foster strong ties to the organization to retain those key senior workers with the knowledge, abilities, and skills needed, who might otherwise leave through retiring or moving to another organization. On the other hand, job embeddedness can be a negative for organizations as it may lock in those who have reached a plateau in their contribution to the organization.

Need for Continued Income

The lack of sufficient income to cover basic family needs such as food, housing, transportation, and health care in retirement is cited most often in studies of older workers as the primary factor influencing their decision to remain in paid employment (Atchley and Barusch 2004; Montenegro, Fisher and Remez 2002). The decision to continue to work may be based on a careful analysis by these older workers of what they need to live a comfortable life in retirement. However, for the most part, older workers often do not plan the financial aspects of their retirement in great detail (Atchley and Barusch 2004).

While retiring to a life of leisure seems attractive at face value, workers approaching the normal retirement age often find that living on a pension or limited savings is not sustainable. While some expenses related to working are no longer applicable, such as maintaining a work wardrobe and transportation to and from work, there are other costs that may increase, such as personal health care and care for an elderly parent. These factors may necessitate that the senior workers remain in or return to paid employment on a part-time or full-time basis (Atchley and Barusch 2004).

The Social Security system and the Medicare program in particular have been projected to face a crisis of underfunding within the next few decades if structural changes are not made to the system. This situation is faced by the United States and several other developed countries (Bowers 2001; OECD 2001). However, these projections of crisis are based on demographic projections of an aging population of Baby Boomers. The projections vary widely and are largely based on the premise that these entitlement programs will outstrip the ability of the U.S. economy to pay for the increases.

Friedland and Summer (1999) have studied the demographic projections of the Census Bureau and various projections of economic growth through the first three decades of this century. Their conclusion is that we are not necessarily destined to face a crisis in our entitlement systems. With only modest annual economic growth in the 2.5 to 3.0 percent range, for example, the authors predict that total government expenditures will be the same proportion of the total economy in 2030. Thus, as they suggest, the argument is not one of being able to sustain entitlements for older Americans, but one of social and political choice around the distribution of wealth among and between the generations.

One possibility to reduce the potential increase in intergenerational transfer payments as the Baby Boomers retire would be to significantly increase the eligibility age for full Social Security. The age for full Social Security benefits slowly increased from age sixty-five to age sixty-seven by 2007. Former U.S. Secretary of Commerce Peter Peterson began arguing in the mid-1990s that the U.S. Social Security system may be facing a crisis under its current structure, if the large Baby Boomer generational cohort begins to retire in their early sixties, to be supported by a much smaller generational cohort of workers who follow. Peterson (1996) called for immediately raising the retirement age to at least age seventy-five to stave off this crisis. Such a move would likely be strongly resisted by those who advocate for the needs of older persons, such as AARP. Another possibility is that Medicare benefits could be limited by increasing the eligibility age or rationed with a means test based on income to determine full or partial eligibility. AARP and other groups have also opposed proposals for these types of changes in Medicare. Funding the support of older Americans through Social Security and Medicare as they are now structured is not, of course, the only alternative. Tradeoffs in benefit levels and taxation to provide lower or higher levels of benefits (through means testing, for example) are always possible. Burggraf (1998), for example, suggests that government taxation policy could be changed to force children to be financially responsible for their parents in lieu of support by the general taxpayer through Social Security or other public programs. Burggraf's premise of course depends on parents having children who earn income. Friedland and Summer (1999) also offer a similar view regarding this tradeoff:

> For example, while Social Security expenditures are large, the program provides the means for many elderly people to live independently. Without it, or with a less generous program, more of the elderly would be forced to live with their adult children. Younger workers may be willing to contribute more taxes to support federal programs if they conclude that the only alternative is to have their parents and in-laws live with them. (p. 59)

Of course, the shifting of more tax revenues to support for older persons may reduce revenues available for other community or social purposes. These views may also be contrary to the trend of parents giving continued support to adult children. In addition, with increasing longevity, there may be more frequent cases in the future of both parents and adult children being eligible for and drawing upon Social Security.

Various other solutions to the problem of increasing intergenerational transfer through the Social Security system have been considered. One solution that has been proposed in recent years is some degree of privatization through the use of a portion of Social Security taxes to establish individual accounts for workers. Workers would be allowed some flexibility to self-manage these accounts through a combination of investment in stocks and bonds. The idea behind setting up these individual accounts is that giving workers some level of control over the investments in these accounts will foster a sense of responsibility for their future with less reliance on receiving checks from the federal government for their retirement (Rosenblatt 2004).

Companies facing the Baby Boomer retirement time bomb could weigh in on this issue. For example, they could more strongly advocate for a higher age level for receiving full Social Security retirement benefits or some form of tax incentive for working longer.

Rather than bringing clarity to the issues, these critiques, analyses, and alternative solutions have often confused Americans and raised their anxiety over whether or not the safety net of Social Security will remain viable when they are ready to retire. This anxiety, if it continues, may have an impact on whether or not older workers remain engaged in paid work longer or whether they would return to the workforce after retirement.

EMPLOYER ATTITUDES AND WORK PRACTICES REGARDING SENIOR WORKERS

There is a mixture of good and bad news regarding the attitudes and work practices of employers concerning senior workers and whether or not they encourage the retention, continued investment in, and hiring of these workers. Moreover, there is considerable variance in these areas across countries. A study by Harper, Kahn, Saxena and Leeson (2006), analyzing data from a 2004–2005 Future of Retirement Study of Organization for Economic Opportunity countries, found that the more developed countries tended to categorize workers as "old" at a higher age than the less developed countries (for example, 44 years in Turkey and 49.3 years in Poland versus 60.4 years in Japan and 57.4 years in the United States). Also, while globally only 35 percent of employees offered older workers the opportunity to move into new kinds of work, 70 percent of the United States and United Kingdom respondents cited such opportunities.

The picture was also positive with regard to employers offering older workers opportunities to learn new skills, with 80 percent of the respondents from the United States, Canada, and the United Kingdom stating that they offer such skill development opportunities to older workers. The picture was not as positive in the area of allowing senior workers to work fewer hours to provide more flexibility. While 71 percent of the United Kingdom employer respondents said they offer this opportunity to older workers, only 49 percent of the United States respondents reported they do so.

On the other hand, the analysis by Harper et al. reflected that the retention and recruitment side of the picture for senior workers is more mixed. While almost 80 percent of the employers responding in the United States said they encourage senior workers to continue working, only about one-third said they actively recruit senior workers to fill positions with needed skills. This was further confirmed by William Rothwell and his colleagues (2008) in the study of Alabama employers. They found that only one in three of these employers had a strategy in place to prepare for the loss of Baby Boomer employees who will be retiring, and only the same one-third had active programs in place to retain senior employees.

One might expect that given the mostly positive data cited above, senior workers in the more developed countries such as the United States would be working longer and retiring later. Unfortunately the data here do not support such an outlook. Again, as cited in the study by Harper and colleagues, the percentage of men aged 60–64 continuing to be actively employed worldwide is over 64 percent, but only 57 percent in North America and 34.5 percent in Europe. The picture is similar for men over age sixty-five, with only 18 percent still actively engaged in the workforce in North America and 7.7 percent in Europe.

WHAT CAN ORGANIZATIONAL LEADERS DO TO PROVIDE AN ENVIRONMENT THAT ENCOURAGES SENIOR WORKER RETENTION?

Senior workers can be retained, fully engaged, and continue as strong contributors to an organization. The leaders and managers of organizations, however, will need to adjust some aspects of work and the workplace to foster continued engagement.

Foster a New Psychological Contract with Workers

Until the last two decades of the twentieth century, workers and employers largely operated under a mostly informal agreement that in exchange for the worker's hard work and loyalty, the employer guaranteed long-term employment and opportunity for advancement in the organization. In addition, in many organizations, particularly in the latter half of the twentieth century, the employee expected to receive a voluntary retirement and reasonable pension for years of loyal service. This agreement, or *contract*, was often considered to be psychologically based on the mutual goodwill of the employer and the worker. While not having the force of law, as with most written contracts, the employee in particular felt that the employer owed him or her respect and continued employment (Morrison and Robinson 1997).

As downsizing, restructuring, involuntary retirement, and other turbulence affecting organizations became increasingly commonplace beginning in the late 1980s and have continued today, employees are increasingly feeling that the contract has been violated by employers (Morrison and Robinson 1997). Older workers have been particularly hard hit by this violation of the psychological contract as they have been acculturated to expect the contract and feel especially betrayed as the contract has unraveled.

Today, the relationship between the organization and the employee has altered significantly. It has moved from a relational to a transactional arrangement where the organization's commitment to its employees may last only as long as their contribution is needed and employees' commitment to the organization may last only as long as their needs are met (Rothwell et al. 2008).

Financial realities in organizations during the recessionary times in the first decade of this century have necessitated a change in the psychological contract, most of which is unavoidable in its result. However, organizations in many cases could have done a better job in renegotiating the psychological contract with employees. This is especially true with regard to the concept of lifetime employment, which most employees have by now figured out no longer exists. The other major change is the concept that an employee can expect a reasonable pension waiting at the end of the work road. In the past two decades, there has been a significant and continuing shift by companies from defined benefit retirement plans, based usually on some combination of years of service and a percentage of high average salary levels. More and more, companies that offer any retirement benefit at all are offering some model of a contribution plan where the employee is responsible for maintaining an investment portfolio subject to much more risk of loss of assets (as has been seen in the recent recession).

Create an Age-neutral Culture

As noted earlier, many organizations in the United States have increasingly fostered a culture where youth is valued over experience, and senior workers are increasingly discounted as contributors to the organization's goals and objectives. If organizations are to retain and leverage the abilities of senior workers, this must change.

Changing the Organizational Culture

The culture of an organization is probably the most difficult area for leaders to influence. It requires continued focus and perseverance, especially if the prevailing organizational culture has not been age neutral. Before tackling the task of changing an organizational culture, it is helpful to have an understanding of what it is. Edgar Schein (2004), the foremost researcher and author in this arena, defines group or organizational culture as

> . . . a pattern of shared basic assumptions that was learned by a group as it solved its problems of external adoption and internal integration that has worked well enough to be considered valid and, therefore, to be taught to new members as the correct way to perceive, think and feel in relation to those problems. (Schein 2004, p. 17)

In Schein's model, organizational culture shows itself in three levels or layers: observable artifacts (such as processes, job design, protocol, etc.), norms and values, and basic assumptions. A complicating aspect of organizational culture is that, particularly in large organizations, distinctive subcultures often exist which may differ from each other significantly. For example, in the information technology department there may be a belief that individuals' skills and knowledge are quickly outdated and therefore more senior workers are, or will be, obsolete. On the other hand, on the manufacturing floor, the more senior workers may be valued for their accumulation of knowledge about how things get done and the best practices to get them done.

In his book, Schein also provides a diagram of the basic mechanisms which leaders should focus on to change culture based on the stage at which the organization exists (see Table 3.1).

At the early stage of the organization, as can be seen in Table 3.1, the leader can change the culture toward age neutral by such things as reinforcing the correct behaviors regarding age by providing insight, by promoting those who model age-neutral behavior, and by setting up

Table 3.1
Culture Change Mechanisms

Organizational stage	Change mechanism
Founding and early growth	1. Incremental change through general and specific evolution
	2. Insight
	3. Promotion of hybrids within the culture
Midlife	4. Systematic promotion from within selected subcultures
	5. Technological seduction
	6. Infusion of outsiders
Maturity and decline	7. Scandal and explosion of myths
	8. Turnarounds
	9. Mergers and acquisition
	10. Destruction and rebirth

Source: Schein, E. H. 2004, p. 292.

hybrid or cross-organizational groups of people who foster and demonstrate an age-neutral approach to operating. At the organization's midlife, the culture becomes more embedded and thus more difficult to change. However, as Schein suggests, there are actions the leader can take. For example, he or she can consciously promote those subcultures and individuals who model age-neutral behavior and/or bring in outsiders who model this behavior. In the maturity stage of an organization, cultural change usually comes from crisis (either real or initiated) or external events, such as a merger or acquisition. The opportunity here is to show that a radical change is needed or to adopt the best of both cultures from merged organizations.

Age and the American Culture in the Workplace

Older persons were once revered for their wisdom and knowledge in the United States, and are still revered in some agricultural and subsistence societies. Even in subsistence societies, however, older persons are only revered up to a point. Sylvia Beales (2000) illustrates this in a story:

In Bangladesh, a story is told of a disabled grandfather who is being removed from the family home in a basket by the son, so that the "burden" of the old man can be disposed of in the forest. On seeing

this, the grandson observes "Father, please be sure to bring back
the basket." On being asked why by the father, the grandson
replies: "Because I will need it when you grow old." (p. 12)

In the United States, older persons have also become increasingly
marginalized as being old, frail, unattractive, and nonproductive (Atchley
and Barusch 2004). With some exceptions, such as those companies cited
in an AARP study (O'Sullivan 2003), many U.S. companies do not consider older persons as a primary source of workers. A bias toward hiring
and retaining younger workers versus older workers has existed in the
United States and other industrialized countries since the beginning of the
industrial revolution. In addition there is an enduring built-in bias to a
youth-oriented culture (Auerbach and Welsh 1994; Goldberg 2000) and
outright age discrimination in some organizations in hiring, promotion,
and layoffs or firing (Johnson and Neumark 1997; Montenegro, Fisher and
Remez 2002; Seagrave 2001). As noted in an article by Sylvia Beales
(2000); "ageism can be detected in processes, attitudes, and behavior
which amount to discrimination through unwitting prejudice, ignorance,
thoughtlessness and stereotyping which disadvantage older people" (p. 10).

The impact of this youth culture is that older workers are often
devalued in the workplace and thus subtly or overtly encouraged to
leave in order to make way for younger workers. Auerbach and Welsh
(1994) see one result of this as dividing the American society and promoting generational conflict. To resolve this bipolarization, they call
for a "new social contract that will balance a sense of community with
individualism and that will halt the movement toward a two-tiered
society . . . a new social contract is necessary to recognize that even as
people age, they can compete" (p. 236).

Shifting to Age Neutrality

During a cultural change in an organization, whether driven externally
(such as during a merger or acquisition) or internally (by the organization's
leadership), it is critically important for managers and leaders to assure that
their human resource decisions are not based on chronological age, either
explicitly or implicitly. Far more decisions in organizations are implicitly
age-based than explicitly (Marshall 1998). The implicit ones are the most
difficult to detect and change, which argues for strong vigilance to combat
age-stereotyping and norms (Hedge, Borman and Lammlein 2006).

Probably the most common implicit age-based issue in organizations
is the prevalence of age norming of jobs and organizational contexts
(Hedge et al. 2006). In this situation, some jobs are seen as younger

person jobs while others are seen as jobs appropriate for older persons. Age norms can also exist around duty assignments and pay levels and other organizational issues.

Floor Slagter (2009) provides a more specific model of an ideal organizational culture which fosters knowledge management and effective knowledge sharing between workers from the generational cohorts in the workplace. Slagter confirmed his model and its positive effects on knowledge sharing in a study of 221 employees in the banking industry in the Netherlands. The factors he cites as critical in this model are:

- Vision that the collaboration between different generations leads to success
- Business and leadership strategy that recognizes the value of the senior employee
- Training, self-development, and career opportunities
- Flexible job design, work-life balance, and health considerations
- Mentoring relationships and intergenerational teams
- Recognition of know-how transfer

How the senior worker perceives the culture in his or her organization is critical to how they see themselves and their contribution valued or not valued by the organization and its leadership.

Provide Health-care Insurance

As individuals age, there is no escaping the need for increased health care, the cost of which continues to escalate in the United States. Many retirees depend on the continuation of group health insurance provided by former employers as part of their pension package. For older workers, continuing to work versus retiring can be partially motivated by the need to maintain health insurance coverage for themselves and their dependents (Gustman and Steinmeier 2000; Madrian, Burtless and Gruber 1994; Rust and Phelan 1997).

The availability of continued employer-provided health insurance coverage has been found to be a significant factor in the choice of male workers, in particular, to retire before age sixty-five (Karoly and Rogowski 1994). As women, particularly those from the Baby Boom generation, accumulate full careers, they too are focusing on the importance of retaining health insurance benefits in retirement (Dailey 1998). The availability of reasonably priced health insurance after retirement, at least for a long enough period to bridge the gap until Medicare is available at age sixty-five, is also a factor in the decision of workers stay in the workplace, or return to the workplace. A cross section of older workers and retirees questioned on the importance of continued affordable health insurance for a recent study for the AARP and information from a report by the Organisation for Economic Co-operation and Development (OECD) supported this view (Montenegro, Fisher and Remez 2002; OECD 2001). The affordability of health insurance is a growing factor for most organizations with the significant rise in healthcare costs over the past few years. Until recently, many organizations provided continued health insurance for retirees on the same basis as active employees. However, with the rising costs more organizations are rethinking this position and eliminating coverage once retirees reach age sixty-five and are eligible for Medicare. This can be particularly problematic for the retiree if the employer-sponsored plan covered his or her spouse, children, or other dependents.

For those persons with private or continued employer-sponsored health insurance who are over age sixty-five, Medicare becomes the primary payer for benefits. In these cases, retirees can often purchase a supplemental plan through their employer-sponsored plan to cover medical expenses beyond those covered by Medicare. However, for those without employer-sponsored or personal health insurance, Medicare would provide their only coverage with usually less benefits, but at a lower cost to the recipient than employer-sponsored or personal health insurance. Thus, the current Medicare minimum age for eligibility would discourage workers from retiring before age sixty-five from an employer who is providing health insurance coverage (Penner, Perun and Steuerle 2002).

Provide Workplace Accommodation

One of the potential factors affecting the decision of retirees to return to work is the degree to which an employer would be willing to accommodate them. This accommodation could be in terms of physical access appropriate to their needs, training, and provision of appropriate technology (Riggs 2004). For example, some older workers may need workspaces that are easy to get to (e.g., without climbing stairs). Also, they may need larger monitors for their computers and software which provides larger typefaces to more easily read the screen, and other assistive technology. In addition, providing health counseling, particularly for weight control and exercise (and access to exercise facilities) is particularly important for older adults as their bodies change in older adulthood (Rothwell et al. 2008).

It should be noted at this point that most of these suggested accommodations are not particularly costly and that almost all employees, regardless of age, could benefit from their implementation.

Another key factor, which we discuss in detail in Chapter 5, is the provision of flexible hours to allow senior employees to balance work and leisure or allow for time to pursue other interests (Montenegro, Fisher and Remez 2002; Penner, Perun and Steuerle 2002).

Provide Part-time Work and/or Some Form of Phased Employment or Retirement Alternatives

Often the choice faced by senior employees when deciding whether or not to stay engaged in the workforce is to continue working at their jobs on a full-time basis, or completely disengage through full retirement. There are other alternatives to this all-or-nothing approach through some type of phased retirement process. It should be acknowledged that the ability of organizations to provide partial retirement or bridge retirement and part-time work for older workers or rehired retirees is currently restricted by tax, age, and retirement laws and regulations. These laws need to be revised and liberalized in order to accommodate retention and rehiring of older workers (Penner, Perun and Steuerle 2002). We discuss part-time employment and other flexible work alternatives in more detail in Chapter 5 and retirement and its forms in more detail in Chapter 7.

DEVELOP AN EFFECTIVE RECRUITING AND EMPLOYMENT PROGRAM TO ATTRACT SENIOR WORKERS

Some companies also have an unstated but often apparent bias toward hiring younger workers, based on the assumption that they bring more energy and innovative ideas to the workplace. The basis of these decisions seems irrational if we assume that senior workers are of equal ability with younger workers and possess the same value as contributors to the accomplishment of organizational mission and goals. What often are not valued in the decision process are the differential abilities and knowledge of senior workers. Moreover, with some exceptions, organizations frequently do not consider the base of retired persons as a source to fulfill their needs for short-term, project-oriented, or part-time work.

There may be a gap in this regard between the human resource professionals in organizations and those in other management positions. For example, a member survey by the Society for Human Resource Management (Collison 2003) of human resource professionals reflected that 72 percent of the respondents said they recognize advantages to their organizations in hiring senior workers. The top advantages cited were senior workers may be more willing to work part-time or seasonally to fill on-demand labor needs, they may serve as mentors to less experienced workers, they may apply their valuable social capital experience, and they have a strong work ethic and are more reliable than younger workers.

Rothwell and his colleagues (2008) suggest that in order to effectively recruit senior workers, recruiting and hiring managers should:

- Understand and mitigate their own age-related biases and identify skills and knowledge gathered in one work situation and make it transferable to the needs of the position for which the employee is being recruited;
- Understand that a perhaps very highly qualified applicant who has worked in a career and/or for another organization for a long time may not be the best at selling themselves. You will therefore need to dig deeper in the interview and be patient in drawing out the experience and knowledge of the older interviewee;
- Understand what qualities are truly important for the position for which you are recruiting and what qualities the older applicant would bring to bear on that position;
- Develop recruiting materials which show mature workers in the workforce and assure that the language in the materials is age-neutral and emphasizes the experience, reliability, and importance of the mission of the organization.

PROVIDE AGE-RELATED DIVERSITY AND NONDISCRIMINATION TRAINING

Most organizations have been providing diversity training for their employees for several decades, to the point that the training has been ingrained in the human resources programs and process. Most of this training has focused on the positive aspects of the value and strength of a diverse workforce, mainly concentrated on racial, ethnic, and gender diversity, and more recently on sexual orientation and lifestyle elements. Age diversity and intergenerational diversity, however, has only recently become an area of focus.

With regard to nondiscrimination training, most organizational training programs and policies also focus on race, ethnicity, gender, and lifestyle issues under the umbrella of the "isms." However, organizations for the most part have developed very little in the way of training programs or workplace policies (other than for meeting legal guidelines) to deal with the issues surrounding *ageism*. As the workforce ages, and the need to retain senior workers grows, organizations will need to place more emphasis in this area.

Since most human resource policies and practices originate with, and are driven by, managers and supervisors, they would be the logical group to begin training on the issues associated with older workers. Some minimum elements that would be appropriate in this type of training program are:

- Having managers and supervisors complete a self-assessment of misconceptions and biases regarding aging and older workers;
- Dealing with the myths and stereotypes and the life changes that people go through as they age, and with the self-fulfilling effects that age stereotyping has on older workers. The program should not be based on the assumption that all older workers are knowledgeable and competent and have all of the necessary skills and behaviors that support the organization's mission, goals, and objectives. On the other hand it should not assume that all younger workers possess these characteristics, and that the older workers somehow have to "close the gap";
- Developing an understanding of the differences in values, work ethics, and needs of the different generational cohorts occupying the workplace. Such training should include discussions of generational differences and how they play out in work behavior (the issues surrounding this area are discussed in more detail in Chapter 6);
- Gaining knowledge of the legal issues pertaining to older workers, such as the bases for age discrimination under the Age Discrimination in Employment Act.

DEVELOP A POSITIVE MULTIGENERATIONAL WORKFORCE

Senior workers and those from younger generational cohorts may find that their goals for work, knowledge of technology, experience, and social and lifestyle values may conflict. This is apparent when working in teams. It is therefore incumbent on managers and leaders to foster effective relationships among the generational cohorts in the workforce. This will hopefully assure that older workers are not isolated or marginalized such that their valuable experience and knowledge is not brought to bear on solving problems and reaching organizational goals. We discuss the aspects of working in intergenerational teams and other intergenerational issues in the workplace in Chapter 6.

PROVIDE FOR CONTINUED LEARNING FOR SENIOR WORKERS

In Youth we learn, in age we understand
Marie von Ebner-Eschenbach (1830–1916)

The Need for a New Network and New Knowledge and Skills

The need for additional training to gain new knowledge or skills is common for people entering new jobs. This may be a particular challenge for retirees who have worked for a long period of time in a single career or field. Subsequent to retirement, they may find that the skills and knowledge that served them well in their preretirement jobs are not current or compatible with available postretirement jobs. In the Venneberg (2005) study, four of the five women felt that they had to gain new knowledge or learn new technical or other skills as part of their transition from retirement to a return to working. For one woman, a geographic move after retirement caused her to need to establish a new network for searching for a new job. Another woman also stated she had to establish a new network to assist in finding a job after a postretirement geographic move. As well, there was a period of time where another participant had to learn new health-care programs which differed from those in her preretirement work. One woman was challenged to relearn some processes that she had not used for some time, and two other women needed to learn new information technology to apply to their new jobs. The men in this study had moved from a federal agency into a consultant company doing business with their agency and others providing a service similar to the work they had overseen in their federal jobs. Therefore, the transition did not require much, if any, acquisition of new knowledge or skills. In fact, one of the men specifically rejected further training offered by his company that was not directly related to his immediate job:

> I said I don't need any courses. Why should I take the courses? I will take courses to improve the work that I'm doing—immediate work that I'm doing. I've done those—I've taken those courses on my own, but I don't need all the other courses. They're for someone who's going to move up in the company. I'm only going to be here for a few years and then I'm out of here.

The comment by the participant may be reflective of the finding in the study by Simpson, Greller and Stroh (2002) that workers aged 40–65 were 70 percent as likely to self-invest in a human capital activity, and those in the late career subset aged 50–65 were slightly more than half as likely to invest than were younger workers. The findings, however, also showed that senior workers were more likely than younger workers to invest in developing *focused* skills that were *job-related*. In particular, those in the late career category aged 50–65 were 1.5 to 2 times more likely than younger workers to invest in academic credentialing programs, targeted career and job-related courses, and on-the-job based computer training.

Plan to Train Current Senior Workers and Former Retirees Who Need Skill Refreshment or New Skills for the Job

There is a popular belief that all people go downhill as they age, both physically and cognitively. While job-related cognitive functioning can deteriorate with age, it does not always occur in all older people. It can also be affected both positively and negatively by other general health conditions. In addition, other factors such as depression, lack of variability in job tasks, and drug and alcohol use can also reduce cognitive functioning, which can affect younger workers as well.

While retirees often have a large store of experience and knowledge which can be brought to bear on the tasks an organization needs to accomplish, some of their skills may need to be refreshed and some new skills may need to be learned. Leaders of organizations need to be aware of this and recognize that older workers are willing and able to learn. However, it must also be recognized that this willingness is often limited to learning which directly applies to the job or task. Those who have retired from a career often are not looking for a second career and often do not wish to learn new skills and gain new knowledge to enable them to move up the organization's promotion ladder.

Training and Learning: What and How Workers Learn Changes with Age and Experience

When managers are considering training and development for employees, particularly for future capacity, it is the older workers who are usually left out. This is largely because of the belief that they will not be with the organization much longer or the belief that they have reached their level of capability, resulting in a "silver ceiling" stopping upward mobility in the organization (Dychtwald 1999). Older workers often need less skill training for day-to-day tasks (except when new technology or processes are being introduced) because of their accumulated experience and knowledge. However, they do continue to desire keeping their skills current as much as younger employees, and are willing to invest their time and effort in developing these skills if provided the opportunity to do so by their employers (Simpson, Greller and Stroh

2002). Thus, organizations may be missing an opportunity by failing to develop the skill assets in older employees.

A range of stereotypes and myths about mature age workers and their participation in the workforce still exist, and serve as barriers to retaining older workers in employment (Bowman and Kearns 2007). Given these negative stereotypes and images of older workers, as well as the prevalence of age discrimination, often senior workers fear that if they train someone else they will be out of a job. Research indicates that older workers possess a desire to go on learning and earning, but in ways which suit their lifestyle preferences. This usually involves part-time work and the availability of flexible scheduling. Additionally, they wish to keep learning, including how to use computers and other technologies (Bowman and Kearns 2007), demonstrating a counter view to the stereotype that older workers are unable to compete in the technological environment of today's workplace. In fact, training and adaptation to new technology for older workers need not be a concern for organizations (Card and O'Donnell 2004). Research shows that older workers do want to learn new technology and are indeed capable of acquiring new skills and learning new tasks (Czaja 2001).

Older workers are open to change; however, they typically learn differently from younger workers. One reason for this is that, in general, they have been removed from classrooms for a much longer period of time and have been using older technology. Older workers may prefer to view, note, repeat, and question a process, system, or technique as opposed to simply listening to an explanation. However, after completing the training, older workers routinely retain knowledge better than younger workers, which results in fewer mistakes and a decreased need for retraining. Because of advances in technology, older workers are becoming more accustomed to the changing technology and learning of new skills than in the past (Card and O'Donnell 2004). In support, results from a 2003 Conference Board survey showed that 72 percent of workers over the age of fifty feel capable of taking on more responsibility, and 66 percent reported that they are interested in further training and development. Additionally, in a study conducted by the National Council on Aging, 85 percent of older workers stated that they are interested in learning new tasks (Kaplan-Leiserson 2001). Moreover, older workers are capable of learning as quickly and thoroughly as younger workers, if they are provided the same opportunity and access to training (Barth, McNaught and Rizzi 1996).

Organizational training and education programs usually are not designed to appeal to the learning needs of older workers, such as hands-on learning while applying, slower pacing, and relevance to experience (Costello 1997; Dychtwald 1999; Goldberg 2000; Howe and

Strauss 1993). Both short- and long-term memory can be affected by age, but again not all people are equal in this regard. Primary memory, such as remembering a telephone number just looked up, and working memory, such as storing information for later use, can be affected by age. However, research has shown that for the most part changes in these forms of memory do not affect work-related activities (Rothwell et al. 2008).

It has been found that while older individuals can learn and integrate new knowledge and skills as well as younger individuals, the pacing of knowledge acquisition needs to be different than that for younger workers. Older workers may need as much as 1.5 to 2 times the amount of time to complete the same training. In addition, older workers seem to learn better with a more lecture-oriented approach where facts are imparted. Also they require more feedback, both positive and negative, and focus, as they often have more to *unlearn* than younger workers (Charness, Czaja and Sharit 2007).

Learning how to use the latest computer-based technology is a special case for older adults. It can be difficult for older workers who have not been exposed to or required to use such technology in prior jobs. Rob Salkowitz (2008) has studied the phenomenon of blending technological learning and knowledge across the generations in the workplace. In particular, he has found that there are eight critical conditions which should be met for technological training programs for older workers:

- Technology training treated as a specific discipline for older adults as it requires different methods than those used for training younger workers;
- A professional approach based on the older learner rather than the technology itself, along with a concern for cultural barriers for older adults and a consistent attention to detail;
- Overcome older adults' fear of experimenting with technology;
- Address older adults' cultural barriers directly, such as trust and authority in collaborative content development;
- Create intergenerational conversations in the learning setting to develop mutual respect and reciprocal learning;
- Understand that older workers will fully participate once they have developed the necessary skills and will be just as excited about using the new technology as their younger counterparts;
- Help older workers manage change. They want to stay relevant in the workplace, and developing technical competency allows them to keep their skills fresh in other areas.

Jerry Hedge and his colleagues (2006) have also developed some key principles for training programs for older workers:

- Conduct outreach and publicize training opportunities and encourage older workers to be proactive in taking advantage of the training offered;
- Focus on building motivation and confidence. Older workers often have a fear of failure and lack the self-efficacy of being completely up-to-date on technology and other skills needed in today's workplace. Thus training programs need to give continuous constructive feedback, provide early reinforcing success, and emphasize the intrinsic reward of gaining mastery;
- Provide strategies for effective learning. Many older workers have been away from training and formal education for some time and are therefore rusty in their learning strategies. In other words, they need to relearn how to learn;
- Use training that is clearly relevant to older workers. Research has shown that older workers in general prefer training content that is directly job-related. They also prefer training that is related to their job assignments to ease the transfer of learning;
- Emphasize the concrete over the abstract. Theoretical underpinnings of the training are not so important to older workers. Trainers should provide the rationale for the training and how it is related to specific job tasks;
- Provide action learning with procedural performance rather than concept-based lecture-type training;
- Use an active, open learning approach. Older workers are more interested in actively participating in the learning provided than perhaps are their younger counterparts who are not as long-removed from the classroom environment. Small group learning also works well for older workers, as do case studies, simulations, role plays, and other forms of participatory learning;
- Model older workers in training examples. In materials and examples, it is effective to show older workers performing and succeeding, rather than just younger workers;
- Provide a training environment that is appropriate to the sensory and physical needs of older employees. They may require larger print in presentations and written materials and higher volume and clearer enunciation than their younger counterparts, for example;
- Ensure that the learning from the training program is transferred to the job by involving peers and supervisors in a supportive role in the job setting.

Design of Training Programs for Senior Workers

Adult learning and training research suggest that there are seven dimensions of a successful training program: motivation, structure, familiarity, organization, time, active participation, and learning strategies (Rothwell et al. 2008). Instructional design for effective training for older workers should consider and incorporate these dimensions as much as possible.

A caution for the reader here is that not all older learners or all younger workers learn the same way. Some are visual learners who gain knowledge more effectively through illustration, models, and pictures. Some are more comfortable with a textual environment and rely on the written word to gain new knowledge. Others may be more auditory and rely on what is said versus what is written. Still others may prefer a touch and feel or hands-on approach to learning. Therefore, organizations should not fall into the one-size-fits-all trap when designing training programs for workers regardless of age.

Motivation

In general, older workers are less likely than younger workers to volunteer for additional training. There is some question whether or not this apparent lack of interest is driven by a lack of personal interest or self-confidence (Maurer 2000) or a feeling that the organization is no longer interested in developing them for growth or further challenge within the organization (Costello 1997; Dychtwald 1999; Goldberg 2000). In addition, older workers may be impeded from seeking further training due to a feeling of inadequacy or fear of failure, particularly with regard to learning new technological skills that younger workers may take for granted. Part of this feeling of inadequacy and fear can be overcome by providing continuous feedback and emphasizing a focus on the goals and objectives of the training.

Structure

A careful task analysis must be part of the design of a training program. For older trainees, a sequence of learning tasks that moves from the simple to the complex and allows for reasonable repetition and practice seems to work the best.

Familiarity

To the degree that trainers can draw out and relate past knowledge and experience of older workers to new knowledge and skills, and provide generalizable examples, older learners will respond more positively to the training.

Organization

Research shows that older learners may have trouble organizing information, particularly that which is significantly different from what they already know. The trainer should, therefore, place material into logical and meaningful groupings and provide guidance on the best ways to organize the new information

Time

It has been found that while older individuals can learn and integrate new knowledge and skills as well as younger individuals, the pacing of knowledge acquisition needs to be different than that for younger workers. Older workers may need as much as 1.5 to 2 times the amount of time to complete the same training. Self-paced learning is often the best approach for older workers to gain new knowledge and skills. Of course, teaching them to more effectively use the time available is an important element of training as well.

Active Participation

Active participation and a hands-on approach to training help older trainees overcome their anxiety about learning. Also, a learner-centered approach wherein the trainees are drawn into discussions allows older workers to share their rich store of experience to enhance the learning experience for all participants.

Learning Strategies

In most training programs, trainees are told what they need to learn but are rarely taught how to learn. Some older workers have developed and incorporated good learning strategies, but many may have not developed them or may have forgotten them due to lack of use. Therefore, a session or two on developing or refreshing learning strategies may be a good start to a new training program.

Value Sets of Older and Younger Workers and Their Impact on Training and Development

Value sets of workers differ, both on an individual and generational basis (Lancaster and Stillman 2002; Smola and Sutton 2002; Zemke, Raines and Filipczk 2000). Thus, effective training and development programs are those that appeal to and aim learning toward those different values and needs.

A characteristic that younger workers from both Generation X and Generation Y share is a need and demand for individualism in how they are treated, trained, and developed in the workplace (Geroy and Venneberg 2003; Zemke, Raines and Filipczak 2000). In addition, both generational cohorts share the value of striking a greater balance between work life and their personal and family lives than their Baby Boomer colleagues (Howe and Strauss 1993; Ruona, Lynham and Chermak 2003; Zemke, Raines and Filipczak 2000). At the same time, training and education programs need to be modified to take into account the different learning styles of older workers. Older workers can learn new processes and tasks. However, they often require a different approach to learning which is more hands on and allows more time for reflection and integration than that needed by younger workers (Costello 1997; Goldberg 2000; Imel 1991). In addition, due to their longer period of employment and often longer tenure in an organization, they may be less concerned about individualism in training and learning.

Several studies and analyses have also reflected that as workers age, the resources organizations invest in their continued training and development begin to decline significantly. After workers reach age 40–45 in the United States, it appears that most organizations significantly slow the amount they invest in human capital through training and education for older workers. This happens despite the fact that these workers are only at the midpoint of their work lives. Both economists who study human capital (Becker 1964) and those who study older workers (Dychtwald 1999; Goldberg 2000; Montenegro, Fisher and Remez 2002) have supported this premise. The findings of a recent study by Creighton and Hudson (2002) of data from the National Center for Educational Statistics (NCES) show that training and education participation remains stable at ages 24–44, begins to decline through about age 54, and then declines dramatically.

It is, however, not clear whether this is a phenomenon of lower organizational investment, a lack of interest by older workers themselves in self-investing in further job-related training and education, or a combination of both. The lack of training and education investment by organizations may also be a result of beliefs or myths held by managers that workers become less flexible and lack the ability to learn and adapt to change as they age (Atchley and Barusch 2004; Costello 1997; Goldberg 2000; Riggs 2004; Schulz 2001).

This decreased investment in training and education for older workers by organizations and lowered participation by older workers themselves may, however, be an artifact of how the measurement has been conducted. For example, a critique by Simpson, Greller, and Stroh (2002) offers a noneconomic view of the apparent lower investment in job-related or productive training and development. Simpson et al. analyzed data from the Adult Education (AE) file from the 1995 National Household Education Survey of the National Center for Educational Statistics (NCES) for patterns of training and education across the life span. They focused their study on both a broad category of workers covering those aged 40–65 and a subset they categorized as *late career* workers aged 50–65. In addition, they used control variables suggested by other literature that may modify the decision of individuals and organizations to invest in human capital: gender, marital status, number of children under eighteen years of age living at home, race, education, occupation, income, and the perceived probability of job layoff. A key premise in their study was that older workers have already accumulated the general skills and knowledge still being sought by younger workers, and therefore rationally focus their personal investment toward technical and nontraditional training which is aimed toward focused occupational skills development. Also, older workers often gain these focused skills through off-the-job, nontraditional, and technical adult education programs, and that information is often not captured in many economic-based studies which focus mainly on direct organizational investment.

Contrary to the belief held by many observers of organizational investment in training and education, the results of the study by Simpson et al. (2002) showed that the degree of employer support for continued work-related education or training did not vary significantly by age of the worker. Workers aged 40–65 were 70 percent as likely to self-invest in a human capital activity while those in the late career subset aged 50–65 were slightly more than half as likely to invest in training and development than were younger workers. The findings, however, also revealed that older workers were more likely than younger workers to invest in developing *focused* skills that were *job-related*. In particular, those in the late career category aged 50–65 were 1.5 to 2 times more likely than younger workers to invest in academic credentialing programs, targeted career and job-related courses, and on-the-job based computer training.

Some research suggests that as they age, senior workers tend to participate less in training opportunities than do younger workers (Cleveland and Shore 1992). Various explanations have been postulated to explain this phenomenon, such as that senior workers are nearing retirement and do not wish to learn, and that their organizations reduce investment in senior workers on the assumption that they will soon depart. However, other factors may not have been considered in this scenario. For example, some research suggests that senior workers may lose self-confidence about their ability to continue to learn (Fossum, Arvey, Paradise and Robbins 1986; Knowles 1973), which may not be based in fact. Others have noted that senior workers are willing to continue to learn, but may not have the personal career planning knowledge and understanding that their younger colleagues possess (Rhebergen and Wognum 1997).

Managers often believe that the senior workers in their organizations lack the capacity to effectively gain knowledge and skills from company-sponsored training (Goldberg 2000). Contrary to that belief, senior workers can learn new processes and tasks. However, they often require a different approach to learning which is more hands on and allows additional time for reflection and integration than younger workers need (Costello 1997; Goldberg 2000; Imel 1991; Stein 2000). Thus, training programs would need to be altered to accommodate the different learning style of older workers. In addition, consideration would have to be given to the different personal and work values of different generational cohorts in the workplace to develop and maintain effective multigenerational work teams and avoid generational value conflict (Goldberg 2000; Lancaster and Stillman 2002; Smola and Sutton 2002; Zemke, Raines and Filipczak 2000).

Career and Promotion: Not Everyone Wants to Move Up the Ladder

In most organizations a career path is understood to be a straight ascending line or a climb up the organizational ladder of rank and responsibility. The line is assumed to plummet to zero upon retirement. However, most workers want to somehow *downshift* their careers into a less intensive but still challenging and rewarding mode. Alternatively, some may want to *sustain* their career trajectory at a level which is comfortable to them but still allows them to provide a valued contribution to the company. The downshifting trajectory is like the right side of a bell-shaped curve which can be planned and accommodated much like the early stages of a career. In the sustaining trajectory, which so far has been more rare, the older worker continues in a high responsibility, high contribution role indefinitely as long as he or she remains healthy, motivated, and able (Dychtwald, Erickson and Morrison 2006). Organizations should be prepared to offer alternatives for the downshifters in particular. For example, in the case of professionals the organization could offer a reduced workload or an alternative assignment. Another example would be to shift a supervisor or manager to become an individual contributor with perhaps a more flexible schedule.

In other words, at some point in their careers, senior workers may appear to show less enthusiasm toward competing to move up the hierarchical ladder in an organization. This may be based on a genuine desire not to take on more responsibility, or because the senior worker believes that he or she is generally overlooked in consideration for promotion. Also, as they reach a more senior level, workers may have found that working harder does not necessarily lead to promotions and salary increases. Their goals may remain the same, but their expectations of reaching them may be modified with experience.

This can lead to a belief by managers that senior workers have "retired in place" and do not actively seek to develop additional skills or enhance their career or develop themselves for future challenges and employability. Contrary to that belief, a recent study (Simpson, Greller and Stroh 2002) found that the key for organizations is to provide nonmonetary incentives to retirees who decide to return to work. Specifically, with the role shift these workers often experience, the following suggestion has been postulated based on results derived from the Venneberg (2005) study: Create an environment where younger managers are not threatened by older experienced employees, where value differences between younger and older employees are valued and respected, and where older employees can effectively use their knowledge and experience to mentor younger employees. All employees, including older employees, maintain their commitment to an organization in two dimensions: *continuance* commitment and *affective* commitment.

Continuance commitment is based on the employee's assessment of the perceived lack of alternatives to the investment he or she has in the organization. This could be based on the direct aspects of the job, such as salary level, title, and role. In addition, as the employee remains with the organization, he or she establishes what Rothwell and his colleagues (2008) call "side bets," that is, those things the employee accumulates from social networks, vacation time, and other perks related to longevity, and involvements and associations outside the organization such as clubs and community activities. These aspects further lock in the employee to the organization over time.

The other dimension of employee commitment to the organization is affective commitment. This dimension of commitment is based on attributions that are made to maintain consistency between one's behavior and attitudes, and on a sense of congruency between the employee's personal goals and those of the organization. This latter form of commitment is also important to younger workers, particularly those from the

Millennial cohort (see Chapter 6 for a more detailed discussion of the needs and values of this generation).

Organizations have less ability to influence continuance commitment as it is largely based on an internal assessment by the employee and his or her development of side bets. Affective commitment on the other hand can be influenced by developing a continuous assessment of how well employee goals and organizational goals are in congruence. While this does not argue with shifting organizational goals to the shifting goals of individual employees, it does suggest that organizational leaders need to communicate the organization's goals regularly and seek feedback from employees on how their values and goals do or might fit.

Retirees Who Formerly Supervised and Managed May No Longer Wish to Do So

As expressed by all seven of the men in a prior study by one of the authors (Venneberg 2005), being a supervisor or manager is a challenging role and takes a great deal of energy and effort. After performing this role for a career, these individuals sought a form of employment which met their needs for working, contributing, and accomplishing and where they did not have to supervise others or lead a program or project. They were selected by their organizations for their knowledge, skills, and contacts without the requirement to use their leadership and managerial skills to supervise or lead projects. As one of the study participants stated:

> I don't want to manage people, I've been through that, got money and I've done better, done that, got my T-shirt, I'm not going to do it again. That's the most onerous part of any form of management is having to deal with the people and worry about their careers, I'm just not going to do it again. I seen guys that I report to here, that's not for me. I was never driven by promotions, it was job satisfaction and today it's still that way. (p. 138)

Notably, five of them also stated that adjusting from the role of manger to individual contributor was not an easy adjustment at first. As one of the participants said:

> I was telling someone the other day that it's really strange, when I go to see a client they tend to stand up for me, because I used to be the senior executive 2nd level supervisor of these people.

So yes, you walk in a door and they stand up. I'm just a—I'm nobody now, right? (p. 128)

If an organization is seeking someone with leadership experience and abilities that these study participants had gained in their past careers, it needs to be sure that further leadership is what they truly want in post-retirement employment. This is especially true for those who have had challenging leadership careers and simply want to be a contributing member of a team in their postretirement job. Senior workers have often reached a point in their careers where they are more highly motivated by valued work and positive relationships with their coworkers and less by promotion than their younger colleagues (Loscocco and Kalleberg 1988 as cited in Barnes-Farrell and Matthews 2007).

Role Shift for Senior Workers: Mentoring

Cummings and Worley (2005) defined *mentoring* as:

. . . establishing a close link between a manager or someone more experienced and another organization member who is less experienced. . . . for older workers . . . , mentoring provides opportunities to share knowledge and experience with others who are less experienced. (p. 407)

Parsloe and Wray (2000) suggest that mentoring supports learning and development of individuals seeking personal and professional growth. They specifically define mentoring as "an exchange of wisdom, support, learning, or guidance for the purpose of personal, spiritual, career or life growth; sometimes used to achieve strategic business goals" (p. 12). The mentoring relationship focuses on the overall growth of the individual, not necessarily on the specific job function or norms and culture of the organization. The effort has elements that are both internal and external to the organization based on the issues the mentee determines are significant.

Mentoring relationships may serve to foster community within an organization and provide knowledge, skill transfer, and career development, for both mentor and mentee. However, organizations need to be aware of and sensitive to issues of intergenerational conflict when establishing these relationships (Card and O'Donnell 2004). Employers should aim to develop a culture of partnership in mentoring relationships and within the organizational framework. The significance of the mentoring relationship is in the learning that occurs and the knowledge that is shared. Increasingly, mentoring is being viewed as not only a one-on-one relationship, but rather as a component of social networking. Mentees are able to acquire valuable knowledge through interacting with and learning from more experienced workers. Mentors help employees learn about and become acclimated to an organization and mentees can seek career guidance and professional advice from mentors (Knowledge@Wharton 2007). Mentoring programs may be a constructive tool in helping new employees assimilate in the organization, learn the culture, and gain an understanding of the political and social issues (Safi and Burrell 2007). Mentors usually possess a solid understanding of the organization's values, culture, and norms, and as such, are able to impart these core aspects to mentees. Older workers, as mentors, often derive a sense of satisfaction from seeing others develop and achieve; they learn a lot through the process, as well (Knowledge@Wharton 2007).

Successful organizations capitalize on their investment in human resources by cultivating leadership potential through integrated programs that accentuate corporate values, critical skills, knowledge management, succession planning, and a global perspective (Watt 2004). Leadership shortages are expected from the Baby Boomer retirement. Organizations are becoming increasingly challenged with succession planning and knowledge retention because of the loss in leadership resulting from this approaching mass retirement. Effective succession planning includes employee mentoring as a key tool to addressing this upcoming deficit (Soonhee 2003). Mentoring programs may operate as an important tool in making this transition smoother.

Succession planning is not just about securing other employees to fill the jobs of those leaving; rather, it involves ensuring that the organizational and job-specific knowledge that is not part of a formal manual or training program is transmitted from employees prior to their leaving, to prevent the loss of valuable knowledge (Delong 2004). Older workers may accomplish a need for emotional fulfillment through work by becoming involved in mentoring and training activities. The opportunity to transfer knowledge, while being recognized and rewarded for this knowledge they have spent years accumulating, contributes to older workers' need to feel valued (McEvoy and Blahna 2001). Additionally, older workers can offer a remarkable example of work ethic and customer service orientation to younger workers (Card and O'Donnell 2004). Good mentoring programs foster the development of intellectual and human capital. Ultimately, a mentoring program can become a central aspect of an organization's social structure (Safi and Burrell 2007).

Employees benefit directly and indirectly from mentoring. These benefits include: (1) opportunities to establish competence and confidence, (2) help in refining communication and other salient skills, (3) getting feedback on a variety of performance and development issues before they become problems, and (4) having a trusted source for information and help in analyzing problems (Geroy, Bray and Venneberg 2005; Ohman 2000; Johnson 1997). Increasingly the work environment has shifted the responsibility of an individual's career from the organization to self; mentoring embraces the changes and growth associated with the individual's lifespan, which also includes components outside the organizational context (Johnson, Geroy and Griego 1999).

In an organizational context, mentoring is often a formal process focused on management and senior staff members who offer knowledge, support, and guidance to accelerate the career advancement of those in junior roles to meet current and future organizational needs (Nemanick 2000; Godshalk and Sosik 2000). However, the role of mentor is not always, nor does it have to be, reserved for managers and leaders. This is true of both informal and formal mentoring programs. Senior employees who are peers or coworkers with more junior employees can fulfill this role as well. In fact, there may be some advantage to this arrangement as the junior employee in the relationship may be more open with a nonsupervisory mentor and the mentor can also be more open about organizational programs and processes and provide guidance on how to get things done which might not always be in the formal channel. As noted previously, senior workers have gained valuable knowledge of "how things work" in their organizations. In addition, senior workers are most likely to have broader networks, both internal and external to organizations. In particular, older workers can serve as valuable mentors for younger employees trying to learn how to successfully work within an established organization. Learning the organization's cultural nuances and developing a network of people within and outside the organization can help younger workers succeed. Thus, older workers can well fulfill the mentoring function because of the social networks they have already developed, and the rich working experiences and the effective role modeling they offer the younger workforce.

Some senior workers may take on the mentoring role informally on their own initiative. For example, one of the themes that emerged from the study by Venneberg (2005) revealed the role shift older workers often face and the value derived for these workers from mentoring. One respondent in a large consulting firm, who was a retiree from a federal government agency, noted that mentoring younger workers was one of his more satisfying, although not official, roles:

> I do a lot of mentoring in this job even though I don't get paid for it per se; I only get paid when I'm working for a client. But a lot of the work is mentoring and helping the young guys to see what the heck's going on and how to—you know, what they ought to be worried about, where the risks are and that sort of thing. (p. 137)

Among the participants, four of the women and two of the men cited the opportunity for mentoring or helping others as one of the things they found to be satisfying about their postretirement work.

The capacity of older workers with experience and knowledge and strong organizational values to effectively mentor younger workers is not always recognized by organizations as an asset (Besl and Kale 1996; Dess and Shaw 2001; Geroy and Venneberg 2003; Venneberg, Wilkinson and Geroy 2004). Mentoring can serve as an important tool for both senior workers and new entrants into the workforce. The expected shortage in senior talent and the critical knowledge lost when these experienced workers retire poses a serious risk to the competitiveness of many businesses. Mentoring and one-on-one interaction provide opportunities for senior employees to transfer the requisite knowledge and skills essential for optimal job performance.

In practice, some human resource professionals have experimented with the development of consulting arrangements in order to facilitate retirees mentoring their replacements. As well, simulations involving case studies prepared by retiring workers may be used as a method to capture vital experiences and knowledge that can be shared with new employees and within the organization. Other approaches to support the transfer of knowledge include pairing junior and senior workers in project teams and designing programs to develop and engage new hires as well as improving their understanding of career advancement within the company (Phillips, Pomerantz and Gully 2007).

CHAPTER 4

Bringing Them In or Bringing Them Back

NOT ALL RETIREES WANT TO STAY RETIRED

Once the initial euphoria of no longer having to go to work each day wears off, some retirees may find that they miss the challenge and feeling of worth associated with working and they may experience a sense of loss from their change in role and status (Atchley and Barusch 2004). In order to recapture feelings of worth, they may find that returning to work in the same or a different field for pay or in a volunteer role will reduce their angst (Dychtwald 1999; Montenegro, Fisher and Remez 2002; Stein, Rocco and Goldenetz 2000). Retirees often reduce their personal level of stress and gain a greater sense of autonomy with the flexibility to pursue other interests at their own pace. However, they also lack the challenge of problem solving and the sense of control usually associated with employment (Ross and Drentea 1998). In addition, older male workers who have continued to work past their retirement eligibility age often have a strong psychological commitment to work and/or have an aversion to or distaste for retirement (Parnes and Sommers 1994).

Not all who have retired from a career or a business want to continue to remain fully retired. In some cases, their motivation to return is economic, as they have found that they cannot live the lifestyle they wish to within their more limited means from a pension or other assets. However, aside from these economic incentives, some retirees return or would like to return to the workplace for more intrinsic reasons.

A study by one of the authors (Venneberg 2005) looked at the experience of a set of retirees who had returned to work after retirement. The major reasons these retirees cited for returning to work after retirement were:

1. They felt they had more to contribute;
2. Their spouse was still working;
3. They missed the social aspect of and mental stimulation of work;
4. They felt their identity was still tied to working;
5. They wanted to stay engaged, stay in touch with their field or do something new;
6. They wanted to continue to receive some extra income for vacations and other things; and/or
7. They wanted a transition to full retirement.

One of the key reasons several of the participants in the study cited for returning to work was that they realized that they were not ready to fully retire because they thought that they had more to contribute. For example, one of the participants who returned to work with a consultant firm said:

> . . . as I grow older I want to think Oh, I can still play with these guys. And if you do it every day and it's working, you're continuing to give yourself some positive feedback. I hope I'm making a contribution that they like. (p. 118)

Another participant said that he returned to work not only to contribute to the organization, but to continue to use and enhance his skills:

> And keeping your hand in is stunningly important . . . And it would be so easy to get out of touch and when you're out of touch it's hard to get back, in fact, you don't get back. So you've got to stay in the game . . . the motivation is the staying in touch. I meant staying in touch with the technology and staying in the game. (p. 123)

RECRUITING SENIOR WORKERS?

Some interest has been shown by a limited number of companies for regaining the potential human and social capital resident in the growing cohort of retirees (O'Sullivan 2003). An active effort has been made by companies to seek and recruit retirees. One notable example is the effort by Home Depot, in concert with AARP, to recruit retirees with specific skills into their stores (Home Depot 2004). Other large retail chains such as CVS Pharmacy and Wal-Mart also have proactive programs for hiring older workers. Some health-care organizations have also been making efforts to recruit retired nurses, with incentives such as paying for their recertification training, to fill the growing shortages of nurses (O'Sullivan 2003). For the most part, however, there are few organizations in the United States actively seeking to recruit retirees. As the pool of potential workers shrinks and organizations seek to reach out to older cohorts for talent to fill critical worker needs, they will have to rethink their employment and other human resource practices.

Follow Unbiased Hiring Practices

In today's fast-paced work environment, driven by rapid change, increased competition, and large scale employee turnover, organizations can easily fall into the trap of discounting or being suspicious of potential employees who have spent a long career in a single organization. Is this a sign of the individual's inertia or stability? The interviewer needs to determine that with the candidate, rather than discount his or her resume out of hand.

Also, hiring manager or human resource professionals need to assure that their job advertisements do not contain loaded words that point to a youth bias such as, "high energy," "fresh thinking," and "fast paced," which effectively say only the young need apply. On the other hand, the use of "experience," "knowledge," and "expertise" welcome both the highly qualified younger and older worker to apply. In addition, organizations need to structure their candidate screening and interviewing processes to assure that they do not put off older candidates. Some of the newer, faddish forms of interviewing, such as explaining how M&Ms are made, for example, may cause older candidates to balk. Psychometric and verbal reasoning tests, while they have proven their value in the interview and screening process, may turn off older candidates as well.

One way to sort candidates down to a short list may be for interviewers to conduct the initial screening interviews by phone so as to avoid rejecting potential employees simply because they look older. One of the participants in one of the author's earlier studies (Venneberg 2005) noted that she was able to secure a well-paying position in her field after retiring from another organization because she structured

her resume on a performance and accomplishment basis without specific dates of education and experience and her initial interviews were
conducted by telephone where she could be free from the stigma of
age. By the time she got to the face-to-face interview, she felt no dis-
comfort about being evaluated based on her age.

Work and Nonwork as a Periodic Cycle

Based on the findings of more recent studies of the attitudes and experience of Baby Boomers toward work and retirement, it appears that
there is the beginning of and will be a significant shift in work patterns of this large cohort over the next decade. Evidence points toward
Baby Boomers engaging in multiple cycles of entry and exit into the
workforce and among careers and types of work. In particular, these
cycles will not necessarily follow a linear upward career progression as
in the past. As Janet Barnes-Farrell and Russell Matthews noted
recently (2007), "Increasingly, workers in their 50s and 60s will
choose (voluntarily or involuntarily) to enter new fields in which they
have no more status or experience than workers in their 20s or 30s"
(p. 144). This is good news for managers and leaders of organizations
who need to capture the experience, knowledge, and skills of senior
workers without having to offer higher or even matching salaries and
benefits or status as they may have held in past jobs or careers.

Gender Differences in the Retirement or Return-to-work Decision

As women have entered the workforce in greater numbers, attained
more equity in educational level, and achieved better paying professional jobs in organizations in the last decades of the prior century, the gap
in the level of private pensions between men and women began to close
somewhat, but still remains (Even and Macpherson 1994). Steady progress was made in reducing the overall poverty levels of aged Americans
in the last few decades of the twentieth century. However,

> Despite all the progress to date, very large numbers of older
> women, both today and tomorrow will live in poverty . . . Being
> assured of adequate income in retirement is especially difficult for
> women because of the traditional sex bias in the workplace, the
> complexity of women's roles, their longer life expectancy, lower
> private pension coverage, inadequate survivor's benefits, and a

long tradition in many families that "managing the finances" is not women's work. (Schulz 2001, p. xii)

Notwithstanding the reality of continued financial risk for older retired women now and in the future, results from the most recent Retirement Confidence Survey by the Employee Benefits Research Institute (2004) reflect that currently employed women and men are about equal in their level of confidence that they will have adequate income and assets in retirement to support a comfortable lifestyle. The exception to this is that women are slightly less likely than men to feel that they will have adequate health care, long-term care, or not outlive their savings. This latter feeling may be due to the recognition by women that they will likely live longer than men.

Overall, men reported a 10 percent higher level of expectation that they would work for pay in retirement than did women. For full-time workers, the expectations of working for pay in retirement were about equal for women and men only at the highest income levels (over $75,000 per year).

Why Would They Work for Your Organization?

Those who have retired from a prior organization and career are not always motivated or attracted by the same things as potential younger employees who are at the start of or the middle of their careers. In his study of retirees who had returned to work (Venneberg 2005), one of the authors found that the pay and benefits of the job were only one of the factors motivating them to select a particular organization or type of work in a postretirement job. Most of the participants chose to work for a particular organization or do a particular type of work after returning to the workforce because

1. They knew the organization and its reputation and the people and/or were solicited by them;
2. The organization values and uses their experience, contacts, and knowledge;
3. They enjoy the work and how people work together;
4. They have an opportunity to mentor and help other employees;
5. They have no promotion pressure or supervisory duties;
6. They are able to work part-time or on a flexible schedule and/ or have some flexibility of assignments;
7. They like the pay and benefits.

One of the key factors in the retirees' choice to come to work for a particular organization was that the organization valued their skill and experience. For example, as one participant put it:

[They selected me] because I had good experience. The pool of experienced people is shrinking so dramatically that they are willing—you know, the company is willing to almost bend over backwards to accommodate your needs. I'm kind of like a senior grey beard type guy who—you know; I've been doing this for 40 years now. They try to match the person with the job so there's very little—you're ordinarily not thrown into an environment that you haven't had some familiarity with before. . . . So, you know the bosses will come to us and say, can you work on so and so, and basically it's— you know, 99 times out of a 100 these are subject matter areas that we have some familiarity with. (Venneberg 2005, p. 134)

Several other participants in the study noted that the work environment and their fellow workers were strong determinants for their choice of an organization to work for in postretirement. As one former retiree stated:

There's nothing down about it. It's a learning environment, they pay me the same as I made before, plus they wanted to give me an increase and I said no. You know, I'm the same as the other people here; I should stay the same as everybody else. Yes, so you know, you just ask somebody "would you show me how you do that?" And they're nice; they help me. (Venneberg 2005, p. 137)

For some, the opportunity to use their experience and skills to help younger, less experienced workers is a strong satisfier in their new organization:

The one that I devote the most time to, there is an opportunity to try and help some younger people out. They aren't always that interested but once in a while you find one that you feel is worthy of some attention and you try and channel them, as best you can, to do the right things. (Venneberg 2005, p. 137)

Why Would They Stay with Your Organization?

As noted in part in the earlier chapters, senior workers have both similar and different motivations for continuing to work than younger employees. The key motivators which can be provided by organizations to retain senior workers are:

- The opportunity for retirees to be contributors to organizational goals, engage in challenging and stimulating work, and maintain a sense of engagement with their work or field of endeavor
- Opportunities for retiree workers to apply the experience, knowledge, and skills gained from a lifetime of work
- Opportunities to continue to learn and develop for improving skills and knowledge for the job at hand
- A culture and climate that allows for social interaction of work for retirees and the feeling of being an important member of their team
- An environment where younger managers are not threatened by older experienced employees, where value differences between younger and older employees are prized and respected and where older employees can effectively use their knowledge and experience to mentor younger employees
- Work schedules and assignment flexibility

Senior workers, whether long-time members or newly recruited to the organization, typically want to participate in further training and development, even if the development is not directed toward future promotion. Mangers can, and often do, mistake this desire for focused job-related training and development for passivity and the lack of desire for further development (Dychtwald, Erickson and Morison 2004). Simpson, Greller and Stroh (2002) found, for example, that senior workers were in fact continuing to invest in their own development albeit for more focused job-related skills and knowledge.

HOW TO RECRUIT SENIOR WORKERS: METHODS AND MESSAGES

Use Your Employees and Their Networks as Recruiting Tools

In one of the author's prior studies (Venneberg 2005) the participant retirees who returned to work, with few exceptions, found their postretirement jobs through a personal or professional network based on past experience with the organization for which they chose to work and often a relationship with persons within the organization. As two of the participants revealed:

> I got a call from one of the guys here, they were looking for some-body with the kind of background I had, so I came over here. I've been here since. (p. 133)

> Of course everybody knew then when I was retiring because they put it out all over the wire and people came from everywhere. A friend of mine worked at a telecommunications company and she was in over her head and she's a good friend, a young woman, she's 50, and she calls and she said, I really, really need you. (p. 133)

Two of those who did not find their postretirement jobs through a personal or professional network said they probably would have done so, but had lost their network due to a geographic move after retirement.

So what does this mean for you leaders and managers in organizations? For one thing, you may have to rethink your work environment and the types of work opportunities in order to attract retirees to return to work.

Promote the Alignment of Your Mission and Values with Those of the Retiree Candidate

Several of the participants in the study by Venneberg (2005) stated that the mission and values of the organizations they were considering for postretirement employment were very important to their choice of employers. For example, one of the participants noted that the alignment of the company's mission with his values was the reason for his selection of the company he worked for after retirement:

> [I knew] the company's history, knowing the kind of people that they've hired, talented, etc. Kind of was a natural progression for me, knowing where they were trying to make inroads and knowing what activities for the government they were trying to support. (p. 133)

The Older Worker as the New Employee

Most organizations have some time of initial orientation training program for new employees. The purpose of this orientation training is to inform employees of the mission, goals, and objectives of the organization; begin their acculturation into the organization; and make them feel that they are a welcomed and valued part of the employer's team.

RESOURCES

Aging and Social Issues

Atchley, Robert C., and Amanda S. Barusch. 2004. *Social forces and aging*, 10th ed. Belmont, CA: Wadsworth.
    A comprehensive treatise on social, work, and other issues related to aging.

Organizational Culture

Cameron, Kim S., and Robert E. Quinn. 2006. *Diagnosing and changing organizational culture: Based on the competing values framework*, rev. ed. San Francisco: Jossey-Bass.
    A guide to analyzing an organization's culture.
Schein, Edgar H. 2004. *Organizational culture and leadership*, 3rd ed. San Francisco: Jossey-Bass.
    The seminal work on how an organizational culture is formed, with special emphasis on the influence of leadership in developing, maintaining, and changing organizational culture.

Training and Development

Moseley, James L., and Joan C. Dessinger. 2007. *Training older workers and learners: Maximizing the performance of an aging workforce*. San Francisco: Pfeiffer.
    A detailed handbook on designing and implementing training programs and practices for older worker-learners (OWLS).
Older Adults Technology Services (OATS): www.oats.org.
    A New York–based nonprofit whose mission is to engage, train, and support older adults in using technology to improve their quality of life and enhance their social and civic engagement. What the organization has learned and what it practices in training older adults can serve as a useful guide for organizations developing their own older worker–specific training programs.
Rothwell, William J., Harvey L. Sterns, Diane Spokus, and Joel M. Reaser. 2008. *Working longer: New strategies for managing, training and retraining older employees*. New York: American Management Association.
    A guide to workplace changes, accommodation training, and learning for older employees.

CHAPTER 5

Work-Life Balance

By working faithfully eight hours a day, you may eventually get to be boss and work twelve hours a day.

Robert Frost (1874–1963)

SENIOR WORKERS SEEK FLEXIBILITY
(AND SO DO OTHER EMPLOYEES)

Integrating employees' work and nonwork lives is increasingly becoming of interest to organizations. Work can enhance the personal lives of workers, and a fulfilling personal life can facilitate working effectively. Work and life are often seen as two spheres that compete with each other for scarce resources of time, money, and emotional involvement (Friedman and Greenhaus 2000). However, there is great value to organizations to enhance work effectiveness with work-life balance.

Before discussing the role of work-life balance in defusing the retirement time bomb, let's first look at what work-life programs are. Although work-life programs are often marginalized as benefits to working mothers, all four generations in the workforce are interested in integrating their work and nonwork lives. In particular, workers want flexibility. However, workers may want flexibility for different reasons based on their generational cohort and or stage of life. A flexible work culture can be particularly useful to retaining older workers (Johnson, Noble and Richman 2005). While many older workers are concerned with reducing their hours, some are concerned with taking care of their aging parents. Some are dealing with both older children who have moved back home and aging parents at the same time. While this "sandwich" phenomenon is usually present in younger generations, older workers can find themselves between generations.

WORKPLACE FLEXIBILITY

Work-life programs were first instituted in the workplace to help alleviate the conflict employees, originally working mothers, were experiencing in the workplace, known as work-life conflict. It has evolved into a concept where work-life balance or integration, when incorporated as a cultural change into the organization, can help the organization become more effective through increased productivity of its workforce.

Work-life programs come in three basic categories: flexible work options, dependent care support, and paid time off. Dependent care support is usually of most interest to working families, but eldercare can be of real importance to older workers. With everyone living longer, retirees may find themselves caring for an elderly parent.

The most useful work-life program available to defuse the retirement time bomb is flexible work arrangements or options. Flexible work options mean that workers have varying degrees of control of when, where, and how their work is done. This type of arrangement is most effective when the work performed is evaluated by outcomes rather than by time spent on the job (also known as "face time").

Organizations implementing flexible work arrangements (FWA) have reported increased productivity of employees utilizing these arrangements, as well as increased ability to both attract and retain workers (SHRM 2009). Almost all organizations surveyed reported that implementing FWA in their organizations increased retention. Many other studies have reported a relationship between the implementation of FWA and increased business performance (Kelly et al. 2008). Although it is difficult to pinpoint cause and effect, the implementation of FWA does not appear to be detrimental to organizations, and can be implemented fairly inexpensively. In addition to aiding in retaining valuable older worker talent, FWA can reduce costs by reducing office space, reducing turnover, reducing absenteeism, and reducing overtime. Implementation of FWA can also increase productivity and organizational commitment, leading to increased worker retention.

Flexible work options include part-time work, job sharing, compressed workweeks, flextime, telecommuting (or homeworking), and cyclic or seasonal work. These will be discussed in turn.

Part-time Work

Part-time work is anything below full-time working hours, usually fewer than thirty-five hours. Each organization decides how many hours an employee must work to be considered full-time. The government also has rules governing when an employee can be considered as part-time. The distinction is important because part-time workers do not usually receive benefits such as health-care insurance. Older workers usually do not need health-care insurance if they are already receiving Medicare or have insurance through their spouse. Employers need to be sure not to allow their workers to work beyond the part-time hours without giving them benefits awarded to full-time employees. They can find themselves in trouble with the federal government by having part-time workers work the same hours as full-time workers and not giving them any benefits. According to the SHRM annual report on benefits for 2009, 35 percent of the companies surveyed did offer health care for part-time employees.

Part-time work can become problematic when the normal workweek is longer than forty hours. If full-time employees work sixty-hour weeks, then thirty hours would be half time, although not considered part-time by federal standards. In any case, part-time workers, particularly if they are recent retirees returning to work, need to be treated with the same respect as full-time workers. Sometimes part-time workers are treated as expendable and not committed to the organization because of their desire for reduced hours. In order to be a part of an organization's time bomb strategy, the older workers who are working part-time need to be treated as well as the full-time employees.

A special type of part-time work is referred to as phased retirement. This allows employees to retire gradually, usually being able to access some of their pension funds to lessen the financial impact of working reduced hours. Employees typically have reduced responsibilities as well. Phased retirement, however, needs to be done carefully, as most pension plans are designed for a traditional retirement where workers simply stop working. (See Chapter 7 for a fuller discussion of types of retirement and phased and flexible retirement.)

There is recent evidence that of all the flexible work arrangements available, the most effective (and hardest to implement) is reducing workload (Kossek and Lee 2008). Reducing workload is a special subset of offering part-time work. An example would be working four days a week instead of five. Pay is cut commensurate with decreased hours. This reduced workload strategy particularly suits professionals who have heavy workloads and work long hours. The reduced load needs to be customized to a particular job. For example, the authors give an example of a sales manager who supervises six salespeople and works five days a week for sixty hours. A reduced load might be working four days a week for fifty hours and only supervising five salespeople.

A CEO interviewed by one of the authors had this to say about a part-time worker who was working on a reduced load basis (Eversole, Gloeckner and Banning 2005):

> . . . she worked for me part-time 3 days a week in a project oriented role and I decided that she was one of my most talented people in my organization . . . I actually gave her a business to run which she did on a 3 day a week basis and we always used to joke about how she was the most productive and efficient person in the organization . . .

Job Sharing

Job sharing is another type of part-time, or a reduced-hours workweek. Job sharing commonly involves two people sharing one full-time job (although it could possibly be more). This arrangement involves the employees sharing both the pay for the work and the accountability for the outcomes of the position.

Although coworkers and supervisors may approach this scenario with caution, it can work very well in an organization. The same CEO interviewed by one of the authors offered an example in his personal experience (Eversole 2005) that a job-sharing arrangement worked so well that he felt he was getting more than half time from each of the workers. Usually a worker in a job-share situation still thinks about work and is devoting some intellectual energy to work-related issues even while not at work.

> I was at a large consumer products company when I hired two women who had young kids that basically worked for me about an average of 3 days a week. You could say they split a job but I was in a strategic planning role so the responsibilities were more task-oriented than they were ongoing business-oriented. The results were phenomenal—my experience was that I basically paid somebody for 3 days a week, and I got 4 days a week worth of work for a couple of reasons: one is because they didn't turn off their mind when they weren't working, they still did voice mail and stuff like that on days they weren't in the office, and they also were more incredibly efficient when they were in the office, because they knew they were only there for a short period of time. (p. 150)

The Flex-Options guide (2007) offers these potential benefits of job sharing:

Two workers for the same job means two different sets of skills, knowledge, abilities, and experience that can work together more effectively and complement each other. It is almost like getting two workers for only one salary in terms of the amount of creative energy that can be brought to bear on organizational work. Each job sharer also has the opportunity to learn from the other, and both enhance their own skills. Since each knows the job, coverage during vacation or sick time is much easier to accomplish and because not every job can be accomplished with reduced hours, job sharing can open up a number of full-time jobs to workers who wish to decrease their hours.

Job sharing can work particularly well as a bridge from retirement. The older worker can share the job with a younger worker, and then a few years later the retiree can leave, with the organizational knowledge transferred to the younger worker. The older worker essentially mentors and coaches the younger worker in the job tasks. Job sharing requires a lot of communication between the two individuals sharing the job, so matching personalities and work styles is important. Usually, coworkers and managers find that two workers can be more productive than one worker (two heads are better than one).

Roundtree and Kerrigan (2007) offer some examples of how job sharing can work. Workers can alternate weeks, or they can split the workday, or they can split the workweek. Splitting the workweek with an overlap on Wednesday, for example, can help ease the transition from one worker to another. Other possibilities are two workers splitting one job 60/40 on the same two days or two workers with different part-time jobs that have a common budget line (Workplace Flexibility 2010).

Although job sharing is a wonderful option for organizations to transfer organizational knowledge from older workers to younger ones, it is still relatively rare. SHRM's annual benefits survey for 2009 surveyed 522 organizations and only 16 percent of them allow job-sharing arrangements. Why don't more organizations offer this option, which seems to be a very effective way to both keep the older worker longer in the organization and help younger employees get up to speed? One answer may be that job sharing is a particularly radical idea for traditional organizations. Coworkers do not necessarily like having to deal with more than one person in a job; managers who have to supervise job-sharing arrangements have to deal with twice as many personalities for each job, which could be perceived as increasing their supervisory workload. Many simply do not have experience with it, and the unknown is daunting. As we will discuss later on in this chapter, starting small by allowing one arrangement and carefully evaluating it and learning lessons from how it can work well usually helps managers and coworkers feel more comfortable. Offering incentives to managers also helps overcome reluctance to try new arrangements.

Compressed, Variable, or Other Alternative Workweek Arrangements

A *compressed workweek* means that an employee can work forty hours in less than five days; for example, Monday through Thursday from 8:00 AM to 6:00 PM. Examples include (Roundtree and Kerrigan 2007):

4/10 or four 10-hour days
3/12 or three 12-hour days
4 1/2 work week—popular in the summer, the employee works four nine-hour days and one four-hour day, typically on Mondays or Fridays
9/80 workweeks—employee works 80 hours in 9 days, taking the 10th day off after working 8 days for 9 hours and the 9th day for 8 hours.

One benefits for the compressed workweek approach includes more days off for the employee, which may be of particular interest for older workers, as it decreases commuting time by reducing days spent commuting and time spent in traffic, and work can be accomplished at different hours of the day when it may be more convenient and productive for the employee. However, it is important to note that this option is not a part-time option; there is no reduction in hours for the older worker with this option. A potential retiree who is interested in concentrated leisure time, for example to work on a sport like golf, may be interested in utilizing this arrangement. As with all programs, the flexibility should be desirable for the worker to entice him or her to stay. However, working a longer workday may not be an option for older workers.

Roundtree and Kerrigan (2007) offer the following example of a company utilizing compressed workweeks. Dow Corning implemented a program that allowed employees to go back and forth from compressed workweeks to traditional hours. This allows greater flexibility in the summer months when many workers like to take days off for leisure activities. Dow Corning even offered this flexibility to its call

center employees. Although a normal compressed workweek is difficult with a call center, it can be done with adequate coverage and
cross training. The company instituted a year-round schedule with
employees taking every fourth Friday off. This example is particularly
important because the year-round schedule was developed by employee
teams.

A CEO interviewed by one of the authors decided to implement a
compressed workweek even though the business case was not there:

> The 4–10 hour work week, for instance, economically, it actually
> costs the company more. It was hard to quantify, but there was a
> morale issue and there was a positive reaction to it and it had
> actually gotten taken away for about a year and was reinstituted.
> That's something where a financial analysis would say, don't do
> this, but at the end of the day, it turned out and I think people
> are thrilled with it. (Eversole 2005, p. 180)

The option of compressed workweeks seems to be more popular
with organizations than other choices. The SHRM study reported that
37 percent of the organizations surveyed offered compressed workweeks
to their employees.

Another alternative is *cyclic time*, also called seasonal working,
which is a schedule allowing for intense periods of work followed by
periods of nonwork. For example, actors work on cyclic time; they
work on a movie or play, and then do not work for months. This type
of schedule also works well for seasonal workers. Retirees who utilize
this type of part-time cyclic arrangement are often called "snowbirds"
because they follow the sun, working six months at a time in two different locations. This type of arrangement works best when the needs
of the organization for extra staffing coincide with where the flexible
worker wants to be located.

Franklin (2007) describes a situation where a CVS employee was
offered a cyclic arrangement. Six months out of the year, the employee
works part-time in Florida and the other six months part-time in New
Jersey. The program has been so successful at CVS that in 2007 they
had 1,000 employees of various ranks and positions participating.
What makes this work at CVS is that they offer health insurance benefits even for part-time employees who work at least twenty hours a
week. Pharmacists, retail clerks, and managers have been able to take
advantage of the program. What does CVS get out of it? Their customers prefer older workers because they perceive them as more experienced and more knowledgeable and therefore like to ask their

advice. CVS also believes that older workers have better customer service skills and therefore can serve as role models and mentors for younger workers.

Flextime

The most widely used flexible work arrangement (54 percent of SHRM organizations surveyed offered it) is *flextime*. Flextime is any arrangement where workers get to choose their own work hours. Usually it involves a core set of hours in the middle of the day, for example, 10:00 AM to 2:00 PM, but the worker can choose what other hours to work as long as the total daily hours remain the same as traditional employees. Flextime is one of the first flexible work arrangements to be offered by companies, and it is the one that organizations feel most comfortable with. Since core times are covered, managers and coworkers feel more secure knowing when they can interact with that employee. It's the easiest one to implement as well, requiring no extra costs to the organization and very little change for the employer and employee.

Roundtree and Kerrigan (2007) note some variation of flextime and potential benefits for employees and the employer. Daily flextime is when the employee works on a regular basis. The employee can also flex on a variable basis, taking time for personal errands and making that up at the end of the day. Flextime can also be instituted only in the summer, when workers may want to work earlier and leave earlier to take advantage of the season's opportunities. This may be particularly interesting to potential retirees who want to play golf or garden. Benefits of flextime include matching hours worked to the hours when an employee feels most productive, allowing employees more control over when they do their work, and helping them avoid rush-hour traffic.

Another CEO interviewed by one of the authors had this to say about flextime:

> I was a senior VP and had an employee who was having a problem with their 13 y[ea]r old son. I found out about it through other people and I approached the employee and suggested to her that she come, you know, that she leave work early enough to be home for her son when he got home from school and to see how that worked and to see if his disciplinary problems would have gotten better and lo and behold they did. So what did that do for that employee? That employee was more loyal because we

were flexible with them, they worked harder, they were more productive because they didn't have to worry about their son anymore and overall I think it increased the productivity of that employee in this company. (Eversole 2005, p. 143)

Another CEO had this to say:

I also believe that there's a linkage, I always look for linkage, and not to be too absurd here, but you take an employee who is able to concentrate on their work and enjoy what they do, recognizing that their job has been set up in such a way that they can get home, and I'm using flextime as just an example here, but the environment has been set up where the company has enabled, where the company is an enabler to allow them to get home, have their time with their family, or have a 3 day weekend so that can have Fri[day] or [Monday] with family. If in fact that translates into a family that feels better about the company, you just won, because you're going home and your family's proud of the fact you work for this co[mpany] and that's gonna help you, that's gonna show up somewhere in your expense line. (Eversole 2005 p. 145)

Flexplace

Flexplace, or remote working, includes any form of work that does not occur at the place of employment. The most common example of this is working from home, or *telecommuting*. The term telecommuting arose originally from the fact that a worker used a telephone connection, either oral or a computer on dial-up, to keep in contact with the office and did not have to commute to their job but could work from home. It has evolved into several different permutations; in some cases, workers are not at their homes, but work in remote locations. Modern technology has enabled workers to get their jobs done from virtually anywhere with e-mail and cell phones.

One special case pointed out by Klein (2007) is that of security. Some businesses handle secure information, so special measures will need to be implemented for those types of homeworking arrangements.

Examples from Roundtree and Kerrigan (2007) include the home office, a satellite office, or "hoteling," where a company has flexible office spaces for employees who do not come in to the office regularly.

There are many potential benefits to remote working (Roundtree and Kerrigan 2007). It is often used as an alternative to relocation. For example, if older workers wish to relocate to a warmer climate, they could continue to work remotely rather than retire. Offering remote working opportunities means that talent can be sourced from anywhere. The organization can also reduce office space costs when a segment of the workforce works remotely. If an older worker has an injury or major surgery that involves some recovery time, a remote working arrangement might help the employee ease back into working at the office. Working at home can also reduce the number of distractions that employees face in the office and can help employees work at the times when they are most productive. For example, if older workers like to work early in the morning, they start working long before the office opens up. It is also an advantage for the worker as commuting costs are reduced.

According to SHRM's *Workplace Flexibility in the 21st Century* report, respondents noted these potential benefits: ability to recruit talent from different pools of workers, an increased amount of diversity in the workforce (for example, workers who are housebound), and satisfaction with the job can be increased as well as loyalty to the organization (also known as organizational commitment). Flexible working means more time spent in their communities, may increase employees' productivity, a reduction in using paid time off for nonwork tasks, and reducing workplace related stress. Finally, when an organization offers flexible work arrangements, it may be able to retain workers who might otherwise need to leave the organization.

Telecommuting can be offered by a company on an ad hoc basis, part-time basis, or full time. Offering telecommuting on an ad hoc basis is the most common. According to SHRM's survey report, 45 percent of organizations surveyed in 2009 offered ad hoc telecommuting as a benefit. This arrangement is typically offered to an employee the organization specifically wants to retain. For example, if a valued employee whom the organization depended on decided that he or she wanted to retire, the manager might suggest an ad hoc arrangement to keep the worker employed. An older worker may wish to relocate to warmer climates, but if offered a chance to relocate and still be able to contribute remotely, may choose to continue to work rather than retire. It is important to note that ad hoc arrangements are provided solely at the discretion of the individual manager. Other employees may not even know that this arrangement is available. Therefore it is usually reserved for the most valued of employees. Although 45 percent of organizations reported they provide this option, it doesn't mean that every employee who asks for it will receive it.

More formal telecommuting options are offered by fewer organizations, according to the SHRM 2009 benefits report. Telecommuting programs can be offered either part-time (offered by 26 percent of organizations surveyed) or full-time (19 percent). While these figures are lower than the ad hoc arrangements, we do not know how many of the ad hoc arrangements are full-time versus part-time.

Ambassadors Group provides educational travel programs in Spokane, Washington. They instituted a telecommuting program after winning an award from the national Alfred P. Sloan Foundation's Awards for Business Excellence in Workplace Flexibility (McLean 2008). When they started their telecommuting program, they realized that they needed to make sure that remote employees were coordinated with the employees who worked in the office. They developed an internal notification policy to ensure that office employees knew how to contact remote workers. They have teleconferencing services so that employees can still have meetings. The company also offers compressed workweeks, but coordinates them so that the same days aren't taken off by everyone.

Employees at Ambassadors Group needed to convince the company that a flexible arrangement would work for both the employee and the company. Remote employees are still expected to attend some company events, such as luncheons or team-building meetings. The company is convinced that this arrangement increases retention of valued employees.

Flexibility also takes the form of flexible career paths. Many potential retirees would stay in the office longer if reducing hours or training successors did not come along with reduced stature in the workplace. Roundtree and Kerrigan (2007) provided a case example of a program called Future Leave utilized by Accenture, a global consulting firm. Future Leave is an employee-funded sabbatical whereby employees can take time off from their careers for whatever reason and then return to them. In an innovative design, employees can put aside 20 percent of their pay to fund the sabbatical. The employee works nine months, and then can take three months off using the pay that has been banked. This can be particularly useful for the older worker with eldercare issues who may need to take some time off to care for aging parents, or who may need to move infirm parents to assisted living, or who simply wants the summer off.

Flexibility can be challenging for an organization to provide. Managers are comfortable with deciding when, where, and how work is to be performed. Losing control of these factors can be particularly alarming to a manager who still is accountable for results. Controlling when and where is particularly important for a manager who does not really know how the work is performed (as in the case of knowledge workers). So, the manager controls the only thing that he or she knows—how long and where the employee works. The fallacy in this argument is that with knowledge workers, their presence at an office is not proof they are actually working. Far more effective than physical control is motivation. Workers are motivated when they are rewarded for the outcomes of their effort, rather than for the time spent accomplishing them. When workers are trusted to work in the most effective way for them, productivity is increased as well as commitment to the organization that allows them such autonomy. A recent study by WFD Consulting and scholars from Brigham Young University and Harvard Medical School provided evidence that both formal and informal flexibility were related to greater employee engagement and retention (Richman et al. 2008).

DEPENDENT CARE AND ELDERCARE

Another work-life benefit organizations offer is assistance in dealing with caregiving for dependents and elderly parents. As many as half of workers have elderly parents to care for, and it is estimated that about fifty working hours are lost each year through caregiving time off (de Valk 2003). Not all workers are parents, nor do all workers have living parents who need some form of assistance. However, many senior workers are finding themselves responsible for helping parents, adult children, and sometimes grandchildren. Employer assistance provided for caregiving includes paid time off, referrals, counseling, as well as extra funds to help offset the caregiving costs. Eldercare benefits mentioned in the SHRM 2009 benefits report include the provision of back-up services if the regular caregiver cannot provide care, as well as providing emergency care for elderly parents. Another benefit mentioned was providing help to employees in assessing what kinds of care arrangements (assisted living, long-term care) to utilize for their parent(s). While 11 percent of the organizations surveyed by SHRM offered eldercare referral services, the other benefits were only provided by less than 1 percent of companies surveyed. The Alliance for Work-Life Progress/ World atWork (as cited by Koppes 2008) reported a much higher figure; of 936 employers surveyed, 37 percent offered eldercare programs. Since so few organizations in the SHRM survey actually offered some of the more helpful eldercare services, the company that does offer them to their workers would have a considerable advantage in attracting older workers with eldercare issues. This is a great opportunity for an innovative company to compete in the war for talent.

Managers and supervisors may feel that simply being understanding about eldercare issues is enough, but a study by Barrah, Shultz, Baltes and Stolz (2004) found that married men attempt to handle eldercare issues with partial absences and benefit from flexible work arrangements such as flextime. Married men may also depend on spousal support when trying to handle both childcare and eldercare issues at once. Women, when faced with eldercare responsibilities, are more likely than men to look for a new job rather than seek more flexibility.

A more recent study by Bernard and Phillips (2007) found that inflexible schedules and too many working hours made eldercare difficult for older workers. Another issue that is usually not considered, and that differs from childcare concerns, is the amount of time driving to the home of the elderly person being cared for, and from the caregiver's home and from work. Often the elderly parent is not living with the employee providing the care. This study found that the informal support from coworkers and managers was more helpful to older workers caring for the elderly than company policies. The older workers in the study were also concerned about the effects on their own health of working long hours in addition to caring for elderly relatives.

HOW OFFERING FLEXIBILITY CAN DEFUSE THE TIME BOMB

Workers facing retirement usually do not want to stop all at once. Most would like to continue working based on some form of reduced schedule. However, inflexible workplaces often force them to make a difficult choice and remove their talent and experience from the company. Providing flexible options for employees of retirement age can help them work longer, or help them phase into a retirement. For example, a job-sharing arrangement with a less-experienced colleague would help transfer knowledge and experience from the retiring employee to a successor. Often, succession planning like this is never an option in organizations that take an all-or-nothing approach to the problem. Only full-time workers are accepted as committed. If eligible employees could transition to a part-time position without losing the perks they would have as full-time employees, they might choose to do that instead of retiring completely.

The key to defusing the retirement time bomb is to help transfer the skills, knowledge, and abilities of the retiring Veterans and Baby Boomers to the other generations in the workplace. This is a long-term strategy that takes time and planning. Organizations are often shortsighted when dealing with employees, figuring that employees are interchangeable parts. In today's complex world, some employees are more valuable than others, and some of those more valuable employees just may be ready to retire. The trick is to recognize who they are and do some succession planning. Currently, succession planning, if done at all, is usually only executed at higher levels. With so many potential retirees, succession planning has to be done at all levels of the organization, wherever talent critical to the success of the organization exists.

BARRIERS TO PROVIDING WORKPLACE FLEXIBILITY

Although defusing the retirement time bomb is simple, it is not easy. Becoming more flexible as an organization is a cultural change effort. Even if championed by senior executives, middle managers in an organization see themselves as losing power and control if employees can choose where, when, and how to do their jobs (Overman 1999). Managers interpret the culture for employees (Magid 1990).

The importance of the supervisor/supervisee relationship cannot be overstated. According to Watkins (1995), this relationship is the best predictor of whether or not there will be issues pertaining to utilization of flexible practices. A manager who is not flexible has a negative influence on employees' ability to use flexible work options, can increase tension, and can decrease the workers' productivity.

Even managers who understand the need for change can be perplexed about how to do their jobs without power and control. They are used to traditional techniques in a full-time culture, and fear losing authority and influence over the work being done (Horning 1995). Managers fear losing control (Mackavey and Levin 1998) when flexible options are utilized. Many managers have beliefs based on traditional theories of employee motivation; these beliefs lead them to regard any requests for flexible work arrangements as meaning the employee is unmotivated to perform (Bruce and Reed 1994). Managers may also question the commitment of employees who ask for FWA (Vincola 1998).

Workplace flexibility does provide some problems for managers (Horning, Gerhard and Michailow 1995). This includes the intensification of the work performed, the increased difficulty of supervision, the increased need to show outcomes as proof of performance, and the possibility of decreasing collaboration in the workplace due to less informal contact. This last difficulty may be generational; Millennials may not need physical informal contact for collaboration to take place.

Many managers are attracted to management as a career precisely because they are motivated by power and control, and need incentives to become leaders rather than managers. Servant leadership (Block 1993) is a concept that has been around for a while, but it is the style most appropriate to providing flexibility for employees. This philosophy is that the leaders, or managers, think of themselves as a resource for the worker, to provide the worker with the tools to do their job, rather than planning or controlling the work.

Managers worry about creating precedents that will lead to demands they cannot satisfy; they worry that using flexible work options will lead their employees to be less productive, and that they are inherently unfair (Bailyn 1993). Managers tend to see requests for FWA as disruptive to business processes (den Dulk and de Ruijter 2008). This is a short-term consideration of the performance of the department. They need training in how to restructure work processes to allow flexibility. This generally involves arranging for some sort of coverage to allow flexibility. They must also take a longer term view of workers in a department as resources whom the organization depends on and cannot lose.

These concerns on the part of managers lead in turn to reluctance on the part of employees to actually utilize the programs. A study by Thompson, Beauvais and Lyness (1999) of 276 business school alumni discovered that managerial support is the most important part of organizational culture determining the employee's decision to utilize FWA as well as other work-life benefits.

Employees fear the negative repercussions of both asking for a FWA and actually using it. These negative repercussions can come both from managers and from coworkers. These concerns negatively influence job satisfaction as well as retention (Anderson, Coffey and Byerly 2002). However, the more power a manager has in the organization, the more likely employees are to ask for and use flexible arrangements (Blair-Loy and Wharton 2002). This reflects the importance placed on top management support to create a flexible work culture.

It is said that training is not the solution to every organizational problem, only the ones where there are a lack of skills, knowledge, and abilities. Many managers simply lack the skills to be able to be servant leaders or to provide their workers with enough autonomy. They worry that treating employees differently will open them up to charges of unfairness. Other managers may not have enough trust to be able to give workers flexibility. Still others require incentives to change their habitual ways of working. This transition to a flexible way of working can be very difficult for managers to embrace without incentives. Employees tend to do what they are rewarded to do; if an organization is committed to transferring the skills from older workers, it needs to provide incentives to managers.

OVERCOMING MANAGEMENT RESISTANCE TO WORKPLACE FLEXIBILITY: MANAGEMENT TRAINING

As mentioned earlier, simply providing the opportunity to be flexible in terms of programs will not change corporate culture. Kofodimos

(1995) found that there were organizations that offered formal policies, but when these policies are not supported by the workplace culture they will not be implemented.

According to a recent study conducted by Ellen Ernst Kossek and Leslie B. Hammer in 2008, training supervisors in handling work-life issues is effective in overcoming barriers to workplace flexibility. They studied frontline workers and their supervisors in supermarkets in America. The training focused on planning coverage and dealing with scheduling conflicts of employees. Self-paced 30–45 minute modules were delivered on the computer, followed by a discussion with a trainer for 75 minutes. Four kinds of skills were addressed in the training: emotional support, structural support, modeling healthy behavior, and partnering. Emotional support involved the supervisor recognizing that employees did have lives, and significant responsibilities, beyond their paid employment. Structural support involved being proactive in dealing with scheduling conflicts by arranging coverage. Modeling behavior involved showing that it was acceptable to attend important family events by attending their own important family events. This is critical since the employee usually watches the boss's behavior for clues about what is acceptable or not. If the supervisor does not model flexible behavior, it is unlikely that the employee will utilize flexible work options. Partnering with other managers builds relationships outside the department and encourages cross training, which in turn increases the options for coverage. This training increased the likelihood that an employee would stay with the company. Employees who perceived their manager as unsupportive prior to the training were less likely to be with the company after a year. Employees of supervisors who had gone through the training were less likely to look elsewhere for work. Transfer of the training was supported through goal setting and recording supportive behaviors.

Motorola, Texas Instruments, Allstate, DuPont, Eli Lilly, IBM, and Citicorp are some of the organizations that have implemented training for supervisors and frontline managers in how to handle work-life balance requests from employees. All supervisors and managers at Motorola have been trained on the company's vision statement (Vincola 1998). Similar to the Dual Agenda approach of Rapoport, Bailyn, Fletcher and Pruitt (2002), managers at Texas Instruments have received training in how to make decisions that take into account both the needs of the business and the work-life integration needs of their employees (Laabs 1998). Recognizing that managers often do not know how to be supportive of employee's work-life integration needs, every manager at Allstate received three days of training to learn how to create supportive environments (Laabs 1998). DuPont managers have been trained in how to allow their employees to use flexible work options (Laabs 1998). Eli Lilly uses a case study approach to teach managers the benefits of work-life programs, including legal issues, diversity, and how to implement programs (Solomon 1999). Recognizing that managers may not know how to focus on outcomes rather than the amount of time put in to work (face time), Eli Lilly has trained their managers in performance management. Harris (2007) noted that training their managers in how to handle work-life issues in the workplace is an important part of their training at Citicorp and IBM.

The following are tips to help managers to create a flexible workplace that can be incorporated into a management training program (adapted from Roundtree and Kerrigan 2007). The first suggestion is to teach managers how to coach employees in how to ask for a flexible work arrangement. A consistent process for each employee will be helpful. This will only be needed for a consistent flexible program; for occasional flexibility it may not be necessary.

This *proposal for flexibility* should include exactly how the employee will accomplish his or her work tasks, how the employee will be as productive or more productive as on a traditional work schedule, and any effect the FWA may have on other employees or on the business. A *review process* should also be instituted that can be used by managers to evaluate whether or not the proposal will work in the current business environment. Companies wishing to utilize flexibility as an organizational cultural change may want to be as creative and systemic about this as possible. Many requests that seem to impact business operations in a disruptive way may actually be implemented in a systemic way with cross training, for example.

Performance needs to be considered. This is an area that can be tricky for managers to navigate, as it involves some trust in the employee. The manager needs to consider whether or not the employee has the ability to manage time and is dependable. Sometimes performance will lag in a situation where flexibility can increase performance. In the case of older workers, it may mean the difference between whether or not the worker seeks retirement. A creative and flexible supervisor can keep an employee working longer by being sensitive to individual needs.

As mentioned in the earlier Ambassadors Group example, it is useful to *involve coworkers* in the decision whether or not to allow the employee to implement a flexibility proposal. This creates buy in on their part as they have had input into the decision. In the case of older workers, the benefit to the organization of retaining these workers for their experience, knowledge, and abilities can make the rationale much clearer.

The aspect of training that may be most difficult for managers is how to manage and keep employees accountable when they are not in the office and under supervision. The focus needs to be on results, contribution, and performance rather than on the time spent in the office. Expectations need to be arranged and agreed upon beforehand. The employee may need to come into work to attend meetings or other work events, and requirements for communication should be established. An example could be how often employees need to check e-mail or call in. With the latest personal communication devices such as the BlackBerry, employees are able to stay in communication even when they are working remotely.

Focusing on outcomes rather than face time requires some trust on the part of the manager. Managers who believe that employees must be supervised instead of themselves being servant leaders for their people will be more difficult to train. As more and more employees try flexible arrangements, managers will become more comfortable with allowing others to do it. This again points to the importance of systemic supports for flexibility such as top management support and performance management incentives. One of the ways to encourage managers to trust employees is to give them financial incentives to try flexible work arrangements. Encouraging a time when the flexible work arrangement is tried out as in a *pilot* is a good idea. Any flexible work arrangement can be tried out for three to six months to see if it is working out. Even if a manager is reluctant, a culture of flexibility requires that the employee be given a chance to prove that the FWA will work for both the employee and the company. Roundtree and Kerrigan's *Flex-Options Guide* (2007), available from www.we-inc.org, has a series of useful templates that an organization can use in developing their flexibility program—which is really an organizational cultural change effort. Each formal flexibility program has its own template with detailed questions that an employee and manager must discuss before attempting to implement FWA.

Part of the training process includes educating managers about some of the myths that surround offering FWA (Rodgers 1992). Information should be presented to demonstrate that just because one person asks for flexibility, everyone in the organization will not automatically want the same flexibility. Flexibility is often perceived as causing problems with customers. Managers also worry that employees will be treated unequally and that this will not be fair.

The use of case studies or scenarios is effective in training managers in how to deal with situations where flexibility is required (Watkins 1995). Managers analyze the case studies and figure out what they would do. Usually the first reaction does not encourage flexibility or work-life balance, so the manager needs to learn that this initial response will not help improve the situation. Creativity is key to coming up with solutions to flexibility needs. Moving away from a mindset of command and control is essential for managers to give up power and control while still maintaining accountability for the outcomes (O'Daniell 1999). As mentioned previously, managers need to shift to a servant leadership mindset (Block 1993), where their job is to help employees do their job. Once a mindset of enabling an employee to get the job done is accomplished, it becomes much easier to implement flexible work options. The manager no longer sees the employee as someone to be controlled and managed, but as someone to be enabled and empowered to get the job done—and giving the employee autonomy over when, where, and how work is accomplished does just that. Managers who do not feel that offering flexible work options is fair will need to recognize that it is no longer possible to expect that the same benefits, policies, and incentives will work with all employees and that fair is not same as equal (Buhler 2008). Fairness means recognizing, accounting for, and accommodating individual differences in workers.

What about managers who cannot or will not embrace flexibility? This is where the company has a choice to make: how committed is it to a flexible workplace in order to retain older workers? Some managers may decide that they do not want to lead this way, that they are more comfortable with the management style they already use. Organizations wishing to use flexibility to retain older workers must make a strategic decision whether or not to allow such managers to continue in a management role.

Management training for flexibility needs to build sensitivity and awareness about employee needs for flexibility as well as provide tools for how to manage the complexities of flexible work arrangements. Managers should experience personal change as a result of the training. In order to create change, managers need a sense of urgency about the situation. This sense of urgency in a training session can be provided by top management. If top management takes the time to talk with their managers and explain how important a flexible culture is to the performance of the company, managers should listen. Managers will not change their behavior, though, unless there is a change in accountability. Providing incentives for managers who are creative and allow flexibility for their employees will go a long way toward changing the culture.

Personal change, according to Peter Block in a workshop one of the authors attended, occurs in small dyads and triads. It is important to build these types of practice-oriented group sessions into the training. The purpose here is twofold: first, to build awareness of how needed a flexible culture is, and second, to get the manager to experience the realization that a flexible culture can work.

The managers undergoing the training session need to be exposed to and aware of two different types of people: workers who need flexibility and managers who have experienced the benefits of being flexible. Older workers who want flexibility can be invited to the session and may give a panel discussion on why they want flexibility and how it would help them stay with the company longer if they had it. After this general session, workers and managers (it is important that the workers are not in session with their managers; that makes the conversation too risky for the worker) get together in dyads or triads, and have a conversation about the realities of being an older worker faced with the choice of whether or not to stay with an organization or to retire.

Once managers have an awareness of how workers who are facing the decision of whether or not to retire think and feel, they should be more open to hearing how others have implemented flexible solutions effectively. If possible, these managers with examples should come from the organization itself; this avoids the pitfall of unconvinced managers saying "it can't work here."

The managers who have used flexible work arrangements successfully in the past can talk collectively to the managers being trained, and then move into the dyads and triads for further group discussion. This amounts to a sort of peer-coaching approach where managers talk about real issues of fear that they face: losing power, control, and authority. Conversations should also take place about trust. Managers will want to know how the "convinced" managers were able to extend trust to employees who requested flexible work arrangements. They will want to ask questions about fairness and how that has been handled. Once managers hear that there are ways to deal with these issues, they will be more open to learning about different techniques that they can use.

After managers have been exposed to the need for personal change in the way they manage their people and that it is possible in their organization, they are then ready to hear some specific information on such topics as how to be servant leaders, how to work with employees to develop a plan for the achievement of outcomes for a particular job, what policies and programs are already in place to serve flexibility, and what are the technologies.

Flexible workplaces require an atmosphere of trust. In his book, *The Speed of Trust*, Stephen M. R. Covey describes ways to build trust in your organization. Trust-building exercises should be part of a training seminar.

Once tools and techniques have been presented, the managers need a chance to practice those skills. The use of role plays, case studies, and scenarios are effective for practicing new behaviors.

Kossek and Lee (2008) described the development of a case study that can create conversations among managers and employees around the concept of reduced hours. In this case study, managers learn about the importance of communication when negotiating a reduced workload arrangement, of closely coordinating so that organizational needs for interaction and availability are met, and of discussing possible challenges such as dealing with headcount and benefit constraints. Other challenges include how to avoid overwork and how to deal with inclusion.

The eventual result of the management training is to "reshape mindsets about management roles and their beliefs about what is possible for managing flexible new work forms" (Kossek and Lee 2008, p. 60). The authors described three new roles that managers capable of allowing flexible work arrangements need to take on.

The first is that of *job designer at a distance with high standards*. This role required that the manager trust the flexible worker for producing results. This role involves being supportive and people-oriented (e.g., a servant leader) but have high standards and clear expectations for performance. This role also required the manager to reconceptualize work structures and allocations which resulted in new ways of working.

The second role the authors described was the *pocket of change collector*. In this role the manager recognized that pockets of change could exist in the organization. The manager considers himself or herself to be a change agent within the organization.

The third role was *proactive big picture thinker*. In this role, the manager looks beyond the one person who wants reduced hours to the big picture of talent management in the larger unit. Workloads and responsibilities have to be reprioritized; work processes get more efficient; more backups are created.

IMPLEMENTING WORKPLACE FLEXIBILITY

As mentioned earlier, training is an important component in helping overcome resistance by managers, but there are other systemic organizational issues that need to be dealt with to create a workplace that is flexible. Flexibility is not really a program; it is an operating philosophy that the company is adopting. Of course, companies don't need to start big; as mentioned earlier, piloting is a good way for everyone to get used to the idea. The maximum benefit for older workers, as well as other workers in the organization, is achieved when all workers feel that they have the flexibility that they need to be able to meet their personal needs while being the most productive that they can be. In their flexibility study, Pitt-Catsouphes and Matz-Costa (2008) concluded that flexibility could improve workers' well-being and their engagement, which could in turn affect organizational performance. This is an added bonus to companies wishing to retain older workers and defuse the retirement time bomb.

Communication

Communicating openly and frequently with employees while creating a FWA program is critical to its success, according to a recent SHRM report on workplace flexibility. Employees need to understand what the program is and how it works. Line managers in particular need to participate in its creation, which creates buy in for the program and the cultural change effort. In addition, line managers need to understand the needs of their employees, including older workers. Open communication facilitates this. Although FWA are usually provided in response to workers' requests, managers of older workers need to provide FWA to their potential retirees to incent them to stay either full-time or part-time, with or without a phasing out of employment.

Successful FWA

SHRM studied about three hundred organizations that offered one or more FWA and considered those arrangements as successful. These companies considered various factors as being important to the success of their FWA. The most important factor for success was the achievement of buy in or support from the top management of the company. Support of top management has generally been acknowledged as being necessary, but not sufficient, for organizational cultural change initiatives. In addition to supporting the initiatives, top managers need to model flexibility.

The next most important factor is how committed the employee is to following policy rules. This signals to the manager and company that the employee is interested not only in his or her own benefit, but is also interested in the well-being of the organization.

FWA can be difficult to implement in organizations, as we've discussed, and some jobs or positions seem to be more difficult to make flexible than others. In one of the author's studies, the job of CEO was described by one CEO as being impossible to job share, while another described sharing his job with another top manager. Call centers are also often cited as not allowing flexibility, yet one CEO described the problem as simply one of coverage. Since call center employees are the face of the employer to customers, this CEO felt he could not afford to have those employees upset at the company because they couldn't take their child to the doctor. In fact, providing sufficient resources for coverage and needing 24/7 service was the next most important factor cited by the SHRM study.

Employees also need to understand the policy, which also means the manager needs to understand it, as employees learn about FWA from their supervisors. This highlights the importance of management training and of open communication between employee and supervisor. Management training supports the next important factor, which is support and buy in from the manager who needs to approve the FWA for the employee. Without this support, the employee will fear negative repercussions. Other studies have found that informal support from supervisors and coworkers is actually most important. In any case, the pivotal role of managers in allowing FWA to take place under their watch cannot be overstated. A company is only as flexible as an employee's supervisor. Employees do not leave companies; they leave their managers. Expertise in people management is critical to employee retention as well, according to Nancy Ahlrichs (2007), a consultant specializing in Employer of Choice strategies.

A supportive organizational culture was the next most important factor. This is not surprising given that managers are interpreters of the organizational culture. Supervisors who are savvy about managing their people and allow FWA actually create the supportive culture. Many of these variables are interrelated.

Other factors found to be important in the survey were how interested employees were in the FWA, how consistent the implementation was (not left to the sole discretion of the supervisor), agreement by the organization on the FWA policies, and piloting the program first with a smaller group and then gradually implementing to the larger organization.

Lilly UK has similar guidelines (Moore and Lockwood 2007). It is important that the FWA are aligned with the organization's strategy. This includes organizational values, the mission statement, and organizational philosophy. FWA need to be regarded as an integral part of achieving the objectives of the business, according to Lilly. Employees need to feel valued and appreciated, which creates an organizational climate that is conducive to flexibility. Lilly also emphasizes the importance of top management support, and the importance of managers serving as role models for flexible working. Additionally, Lilly stresses the importance of training and providing tools for managers to be able to provide flexible programs to staff.

A study by Koc-Menard (2009) of older workers in Europe and North America identified three important lessons for adopting FWA for older workers in order to attract and retain them. The first recommendation is that a portfolio of work flexibility options should be used, offering different combinations. The second recommendation is to align FWA for retirees with pension scheme options. Rafter (2008) notes that in the United States, workers can start collecting partial pension payments while they continue working after the age of sixty-two. This option, however, needs to exercised with care, as it is subject to pension reform laws passed in 2006. The legislation was intended to accommodate retirees who wanted to work reduced hours and start drawing from their pension, but confusion around the laws means that companies are not making these programs formal but leaving them informal. The regulations did not affect 401(k)s, as potential retirees can work reduced hours at 59 $1/2$ and still withdraw funds to replenish lost earnings. Finland is an example of a country where workers can reduce their hours 30–70 percent of full time while receiving partial payments from their plan (Hegewisch and Gornick 2008). What is eventually permitted by the government may not be the same as what organizations will allow, and neither of these options may be what will convince older workers to stay longer in the workplace (Kelly, Dahlin, Spencer and Moen 2008). Organizations would be wise to continue to work with the federal government to figure out ways to enable workers to reduce their hours rather than retiring full time.

Measuring Success

When implementing FWA, it is important to measure successes. According to SHRM (2009), few organizations that offered FWA actually measured how successful they were. By measuring and communicating successes, the organization can help persuade other managers and older workers that work for them that FWA can be a successful alternative to retirement. This will also help change the corporate culture so that flexibility is seen as a viable alternative for employees.

The report provided several ideas for how to measure the effectiveness of telework. Out of 164 organizations that provided telework options, almost half noted the importance of establishing specific goals with the employee. A third of the companies surveyed used employee progress reports with schedules and task assignments. Time can also be recorded on timesheets, logbooks, or with computer tracking software. Older workers tend to be experienced and knowledgeable about job tasks, so it makes sense to allow them the flexibility to do their jobs with a maximum amount of autonomy and a focus on outcomes, rather than time spent on the job. Negotiating outcomes is critical to success of telework.

Johnson et al. (2005) provides some other measurement and analysis ideas. Surveys and opinion gathering methods such as focus groups can measure how employees feel about flexible work arrangements that are offered. Measurements of utilization rates can also be useful. Users of FWA can be compared to employees who do not use them and workers profiled with and without flexibility. Flexibility can be correlated to health outcomes, retention, and commitment. Units of analysis can include the business, status of job, or demographics of the workers. The FWA types can be tracked and assessed. Overtime, retention, cycle time, increased coverage, and customer satisfaction can be tracked with and without flexibility. Evaluations such as a 360 can measure opinions of employees and workers, and employees and coworkers can report the effects of flexibility. If there is a flexibility website, interest in flexibility can be tracked by hits.

AN ORGANIZATIONAL CULTURAL CHANGE APPROACH

Koppes (2008) described another framework for changing workplace culture to be more flexible and supportive of work-life integration. The first phase is to get organizational support and buy in from stakeholders and link flexibility to business outcomes. In the case of older workers, flexibility would be linked to the goal of reducing the impact on the organization of retirees leaving a talent gap. The next phase is the development of a task force representative of the organization to conduct a needs assessment and surface strategies and solutions. Step three is to conduct the needs assessment.

The needs assessment will do a gap analysis of existing policies, programs, benefits, and culture. Existing conditions are compared with best practices. Next, diverse focus groups collate the issues involved in addressing the gaps. The third step is to survey the company to elicit its work-life culture. Then the culture can be benchmarked, demographic data of the workforce reviewed, resources identified both internal and external to the company, and the results summarized.

The last two phases are to recommend strategies and solutions and then obtain approval. The approval process usually involves a presentation of findings and recommendations to top management. Employee stories can be recorded and played back to the executives to put faces on the issue.

FLEXIBILITY FOR LOWER-WAGE WORKERS

Although knowledge workers are able to work from almost anywhere, some kinds of jobs need to be performed at the place of employment. Nonetheless, all workers can be afforded some type of flexibility in their working hours by providing enough coverage. For example, in a call center, a worker can be allowed the flexibility to go to the doctor with a sick child if there is a "floater" who is able to temporarily do the job while the worker attends to personal business. It is this type of emergency flexibility that is most valued by workers and provides the most loyalty to the employer who offers it. Enabling an employee to take time off for personal emergencies without loss of pay or losing the job itself can be another form of workplace flexibility.

Most workers who get flexibility are knowledge workers whose output can be measured objectively. Another reason that flexibility is usually reserved for more talented workers is that when justified in order to reduce turnover costs (for example, when older workers leave), more highly paid workers have a greater return for the organization (Kelly et al. 2008). For workers who cannot do their jobs anywhere but at the workplace, companies can still be flexible. In some ways, it is even more important to be flexible with lower-wage workers because they are the workers who interface directly with the customer. They can have a large impact on how the organization is perceived by the public. Customer service and retail employees tend to treat their customers the way that they are treated. The costs of turnover for these employees may not be as high as professional workers, but there are tremendous costs when poor customer service drives customers away.

Perhaps the most telling example from one of the authors' research is the stark difference between CEOs who have a flexible mindset and those who do not. While it is generally felt that there are some jobs that cannot be flexible, for example call centers, flexible CEOs (and managers!) can even build in flexibility into those jobs. While one CEO told the author that he could not provide flexibility in his company's call centers, another said that the call center was one place that flexibility was crucial because it was staffed by frontline employees. These were the last people that the company wanted to feel unappreciated and undervalued!

> . . . by definition there are going to be a certain percentage of people who are not going to be able to come in a certain day and one of the things you do if you staff call centers well is you build in that coverage. (Eversole 2005, p. 144)

In 2006, Joan Williams wrote a paper entitled "One Sick Child Away from Being Fired," about the plight of hourly workers who do not have enough scheduling flexibility to be able to stay home for a sick child (Williams 2006). Williams' report leaves no doubt that inflexible business practices are bad for business. They result in staffing vacancies that disrupt business, angry workers, and loss of productivity. Hourly workers are less likely to use—or have available to them—flexible work arrangements, yet their needs are just as great, or greater, than professionals. Organizations need to put in place cross training and backup in the form of floaters to flexibly staff frontline employee ranks. This is not new for some industries; medical workplaces and the airlines use flexible scheduling all the time. The common perception is that flexibility is something only for workers who are paid enough and can negotiate with their supervisor a suitable FWA. This highlights the importance of a flexible work culture that makes flexibility available to all employees.

COMPANIES THAT HAVE MADE FLEXIBILITY WORK

A SHRM report, *Work/Life Balance Series: A Global Perspective* (available from SHRM.org), written by Moore and Lockwood (2007) offers IBM as an example of global companies that have made flexibility work. The most important of IBM's work-life balance initiatives are based on flexibility. A survey from 2004 of 98,000 employees in seventy-nine countries showed that flexibility had increased dramatically. Employees rated their work-life balance satisfaction higher than three years prior and said that telework had been a positive influence. Ninety percent of employees working from home reported an increase in productivity. To read more about IBM's experience, see Hill, Jackson and Martinengo (2006).

Costco is another organization that uses flexible scheduling as well as higher compensation and their turnover is far below that of their competitors (Levin-Epstein 2006). Johnson et al. (2005) offers more examples of how flexibility has helped organizations attract and retain valued workers. Accenture found in a recent survey of its employees about their work-life programs that their ability to balance their work and personal lives had been a factor in the decision to stay at the company for 80 percent of them. Flexibility was considered on par with compensation and career advancement as motivators. This study helped convince Accenture that providing flexibility was good for their business and therefore should be spread more widely throughout the organization. Ernst and Young also surveyed their employees and found that turnover was affected by their employees' perception that they had the amount of flexibility they required. Even though 83 percent of the employees thought that the company provided enough flexibility, 20 percent considered leaving as a result of perceiving they did not have the flexibility required. AstraZeneca also surveyed their employees and found that 96 percent of their employees considered flexibility a factor in whether or not to stay at the company.

Tahmincioglu (2007) reported on a couple of examples of companies and their use of flexible work arrangements. Sun has what they call an Open Work program. Employees have three choices of where to work. They can work out of an assigned on-site office, they can work out of a remote office, or they can work at home. This program has saved Sun $387 million in real estate and information technology costs. While a hotel concierge does not seem like a job that could be done remotely, the Hyatt Regency in Santa Clara has done just that. In a case where thinking outside the box helped retain a valued worker, the concierge works out of her home and guests see her on a webcam.

Although there is no guarantee that flexibility will help any one individual company, there are many companies that have been convinced that flexibility is an option that can help in retaining valuable employees, including older workers. For more examples, see a report, "Overcoming the Implementation Gap," by Boston College's Center for Work and Family (Van Deusen, James, Gill and McKechnie 2008).

Added Benefit of Flexibility: Better Health Outcomes

There is a growing body of research that has been able to link flexible workplace cultures with increased employee health outcomes. A longitudinal study by Casey and Grzywacz (2008), of the Wake Forest University School of Medicine, found that over time, as flexibility available to the worker increased, absences due to sickness decreased as did impairments related to work (work being affected by the health of the worker, for example). Also, the researchers found that commitment to the job improved over a one-year period. This study is important because it suggests that not only can flexibility help companies retain older workers, it can also help the organization cut health-care costs. This considerably improves the return on investment, particularly of the more costly types of flexibility (for example, setting up remote office space and hiring additional staff to provide more backup).

In a similar study, workers engaged in formal flexible work arrangements were found to have less stress and less burnout (Grzywacz, Carlson and Shulkin 2008). Flextime seemed to be the most effective at reducing stress and burnout.

View from the Top

As mentioned previously, top management support is critical for the development of a flexible work culture. Here is a sampling of quotes from CEOs who have been flexible with their employees and how valuable they felt this flexibility was (interview data, Eversole 2005):

We expect a lot from people from a work point of view, but if we give them completely rigid rules to work by and that doesn't work in their real life, then they aren't going to be terribly productive. So we don't have a ton of statistics that measure that, we can't say because of flexibility we offer employees, the managers, to make these kind of decisions that we get more productivity than other folks but intuitively it seems to me it's the case. We have historically very, very, low turnover rate averaging in the 2–3% a year range for most of our history and we have looked at formalizing programs and we have decided in each case not to do it. (pp. 143–144)

The way I think of it is less formal flex programs to adjust to a specific family need and more that's being a professional staff member. It means if you've got a child conference today, you've got a conference, if you need to come in later forever because of you're getting the kids to school in the morning and it takes you a while to do that, that's fine and as long as you're getting your job done and adjusting to that I don't care. (p. 143)

It just made good business sense, it just never made sense to me to try and not be accommodating as it related to a tradeoff for either productivity or engagement in what we're trying to get done. So much of it, I think is just a tolerance or understanding or realization that you could be flexible and still be successful. (p. 143)

As long as the job gets done and the person is a contributing member of the team and a valued member of the team in terms of their work product and output, we're gonna make whatever arrangements keep that employee happy because the bottom line is without happy employees who feel they are treated fairly and equitably across the whole organization you won't have a successful company. (p. 145)

This approach (work/family programs) is a phenomenally positive thing to do as a leader of a company and I think people who don't

do this are blind and ignorant and unwilling to be flexible and
I'm not sure I'd want to work in a place like that, even me.
(p. 148)

In conclusion, workplace flexibility is a valuable tool to retain older
workers who are considering retirement. There are many resources
available for employers to institute both formal and informal flexibility
into their organizations. While it is best to have a flexible work culture that provides flexibility for all workers, ad hoc arrangements can
be made by managers who have a flexible mindset to retain talented
workers the organization otherwise would lose to retirement. Even if
top management is convinced that flexibility is good for defusing the
retirement time bomb, middle level managers fearful of losing power
and control may not be able to implement the flexible work strategy
without some sort of training in how to handle the arrangements.
Although organizations may be offering flexible work arrangements,
employees still may not use them or their supervisors may not allow
them to use them. Although the Alliance for Work-Life Progress
surveyed over 900 U.S. employers and found that 75 percent of them
offered flexible work arrangements, that does not translate to most
workers actually using flexibility (as cited in Koppes 2008). The number of employees who actually use flexibility would be a more useful
statistic, but that is more difficult to find. Finally, organizations that
have become more flexible have reaped the benefits of increased
productivity as well as increased retention of valued older workers.

CHAPTER 6

Dealing with the Multiple Generations in the Workforce

WHY CAN'T WE GET ALONG?

The following comments were found in an online forum on the conflicts between the generations at work started by Jim Heskett (2007):

> This article seems to say more about the expectations of aging Baby Boomer managers than it does about the "millennial generation." There is a tinge of a hazing theme expressed as if to say "this generation must endure boring, tedious, seemingly meaningless work without explanation because I had to." Doesn't this run counter to business realities in the 21 century? Doesn't it say in Collins' *Good to Great* that it's more important to ask what shouldn't be done than what should be? Of course millennials want instant gratification. Who doesn't? That's not to say they can't or won't delay their gratification when called upon. I believe it is up to managers to serve, to work on behalf of those who work for them. As such, it's important for those managers to provide some logotherapy to their subordinates, to provide meaning for their "suffering." Too often I witness managers, managing out of defense of their position or title and not of their ability or desire to serve and produce the deliverables of quality leadership. I welcome the influx of millennials into the workforce and the ranks of management. They at least know how to type and utilize technology unlike many aging Baby Boomers. (Heskett 2007)

The millennials have no staying power as their shelf life is rather short. They have no long term commitment or loyalty to organizations and unless they are fast tracked, overtime, they slow down and want out especially when they feel misunderstood or unappreciated. (Heskett 2007)

As these comments above illustrate, there seems to be some actual or perceived friction between older and younger workers in the workforce. Stereotypes of the four generations abound. Proponents of the generational cohort theory of Howe and Strauss (2000) debate with others in the organization who don't think the younger workers are any different than older workers were when they first started out in their organizations. According to Jean Twenge, author of *Generation Me*, "60% of employers say that their workplaces suffer from tension among the generations" (2006, p. 217).

As noted in Chapter 1, the workplace today has workers from four different generations. This is the result of the population living longer and the tendency of older workers to delay retirement and keep working. Certainly, the economic necessity of working longer is also a factor. The Veterans and Baby Boomers have not yet retired, and Generation X and the Millennials are waiting for older workers to retire so that they can advance in their careers. There is a concern among organizations that the Millennials aren't ready to take over, and there are too few Gen X workers to take over for the aging Boomers and Veterans perched on the edge of retirement. There is also a sense that workers from younger generations do not have the same mindset as the employees poised to retire.

Theorists, researchers, and authors have developed several delineations of the demarcation of the generations. It is important to note that the cutoff may be sooner or later, and people born on the cusp between generations can have characteristics from both. To avoid confusion, the following are the generations and years they were born that we are using for this book:

Veterans: Born just before and during WWII, small number of workers
Baby Boomers: 1946–1964, about 76 million strong, the oldest turning 65 in 2011
Generation X: 1965–1979, 51 million
Millennials: 1980–1995, 70 million

While stereotyping people is never a good idea, there do seem to be some general differences in the way that older and younger workers behave in the workplace. Human resource managers in organizations have noticed some differences. SHRM conducted a study on generational differences in the workforce (Burke 2004). They found a number of factors that resulted in conflicts among the generations. These included the areas of work ethics, organizational hierarchy, and change management. Respondents made comments that showed that older workers perceived that younger generations did not want to work as hard and put in the same kind of effort and time that older workers would. Senior workers felt that they were more dedicated to work than their counterparts, who thought results mattered more than time put in. This study highlights one of the major issues between generations in the workplace. They simply view what it means to be a valued employee differently. For older workers, time is the most meaningful indicator of workplace commitment. This insistence has led the workplace in the direction of holding face time in such regard. If you care about work, you put your time in to your job. Younger workers want to focus on getting results, rather than the time put in to the work. Output means more to them than how much time it took to get their results. Harris (2007) offered the example of the employee who leaves at 5:00 PM to attend to personal matters, but is back at 8:00 PM in front of the computer working late. Older workers don't see the work that is performed outside of normal working hours. Younger employees do not want to be told what to do, want to be judged based on outcomes, want better pay for better work, and want complete flexibility in how they do their jobs.

Another area of potential conflict between older and younger generations is in how they view bureaucratic organizations. Older workers worked their way up the ranks and put in their time. They feel that their seniority entitles them to be promoted into the jobs that they want. Younger workers believe that qualifications alone should result in getting jobs, and resist the authority that comes with age. They do not feel that it is a problem to bypass the chain of command. Respect needs to be earned rather than garnered by virtue of time put in. Lancaster and Stillman (2002) noted that each generation viewed the chain of command differently. Boomers want to change the chain of command, and Generation X simply wants the autonomy to be able to direct their own work (self-command). Finally, Millennials want to be able to share and collaborate—no commanding required at all.

The stereotype of older workers being unable to quickly change the way that they do things is also a source of conflict in the workplace. While older workers don't necessarily lack the kinds of skills that younger generations have in abundance in new technologies, they don't like the tendency of the younger generation to question everything as a matter of course. Millennials in particular have been raised by their parents to be active participants in home life; they expect to do the same at work. When they aren't able to participate and have their ideas considered, they are ready to leave and try again somewhere else. To older generations, this seems like disloyalty, but Millennials are not loyal to their organizations. They have been told repeatedly that they will not stay with the same organization and even not with the same career, so being loyal to one organization simply does not make sense (Buahene and Kovary 2007).

One Millennial had this to say about loyalty (Heskett 2007):

> Loyalty is an interesting point. Loyalty is a process involving two parties. I will bend over backwards for a company who will reciprocate the effort and often we like to think that companies will make extra efforts to retain valuable employees. The culprit for the demise of loyalty I think is change. Today's corporations need to adapt to a fast moving consumer market which is very volatile and to be successful they need to undergo constant transformation to be able to keep up the pace. That change applies to everything including the workforce. More and more, employees have become a marketable commodity and have become expendable when necessary. Individuals have therefore needed to adapt to that concept and therefore we have gone out to find and maintain the marketable skills which themselves are constantly changing. As a result you end up with a "learn and go" workforce constantly on the move to keep up. Essentially it's a bit of a vicious circle.

Shifting Values

Boomers and Veterans had a different employment contract than younger generations. Older workers knew if they worked hard, they would be rewarded with job stability. Gen X has never had this belief, nor the expectation that loyalty would be rewarded with stability. They saw their parents lose their jobs; they saw their parents divorce; they were latchkey kids. These workers are more cynical and more likely to leave an organization to find a better fit elsewhere. Consider that the average Boomer stayed in a job for fifteen years in 1980 and ten years in 2000, while for Generation X that job tenure fell to five years, according to the U.S. Bureau of Labor Statistics.

Burke (2004) found the following traits for each of the generations: The Veterans like to have a long tenure at an organization, respect the hierarchy or chain of command, enjoy structure, accept authority, and give the maximum of effort. On the other end of the spectrum, the Millennials are more technologically capable, comfortable with diversity, are quick learners, but need supervision. This shows that the two extremes of the generational divide have different characteristics in the workplace.

Emotional intelligence may also be a factor in differences between older and younger workers. TalentSmart, a consulting company that researches emotional intelligence in the workplace, has found that self-management increases with age (Thomas, Tasler and Su 2008). This appears to be true even within generations. The authors conclude that younger workers will eventually develop self-management skills as they age, rather than lack of self-management being a permanent trait of these specific younger generations.

While historians and sociologists have been at the forefront of the generational cohort theory, scholars who study the workplace are not convinced that these differences actually exist. Johnson and Lopes (2008) argue that there is little evidence that younger workers are really much different than older workers. The truth probably lies somewhere in between. All employees are less loyal because of the changing employment contract. Two defining experiences that may have an effect in the workplace is the way that the generations grew up. Millennials grew up being equal partners in their families; they now expect the same in the workplace. Millennials grew up with instant access to information; they expect the same in organizations when they get there, and are disappointed with the slow pace of the work environment. They may not realize at first that the lack of speed in organizations is due to complexity as well as bureaucracy. On the other hand, due to their facility with the Internet, they may be more adaptable, which is just what organizations need today.

The Center for Creative Leadership also questions whether these generational differences actually exist (Deal, as cited in Fraone, Hartmann and McNally n.d.). The areas where they found differences included showing respect, how to give and receive feedback, and learning styles.

For the purposes of this chapter, we will not argue the technical point of whether generational theory is actually true or not. We do not intend to stereotype by using the terms for different generations of workers. The terms are useful as general guides with the caveat that no one person born at a particular time will have particular traits. As a broad generalization though, there are differences in the way workers interact with each other based at least on their tenure in the workforce.

Benefits and Challenges of Multiple Generations Working Together

The intergenerational workforce may be conceptualized as age diversity (Pitt-Catsouphes 2007). This approach notes that age does not necessarily correlate with a generational cohort, and it may instead be more meaningful to look at from career stages. Employees in these diverse career stages bring different strengths to the workplace. Taking an age diversity approach, employees are either in the early, middle, or late career stages. Early career individuals tend to be more creative and take more initiative, while late career employees are more loyal and reliable and have networks of professional colleagues and clients, a high level of skill, a strong work ethic, and low turnover. Late career employees seem to be quite similar to Veteran or Boomer groups; however, if an older worker is just starting out in a career, he or she may not have the same characteristics in the workplace as other older workers. In working with the intergenerational workforce, it is wise to avoid stereotyping.

The important thing is to learn to try to get along and respect each other's individual differences. Dealing with diversity is just good managerial practice. When the workforce was more homogeneous, managers could get away with managing in more traditional ways. Now the workforce is so diverse, a good manager has to be creative and flexible to be able to deal with multiple issues. Managers also need to have good interpersonal skills.

Fraone (n.d.) noted the main challenges that organizations face are due to perceptions and stereotypes of the different generations, rather than the characteristics themselves. Three areas where the challenges are concentrated are perspectives on work, communication between generations, and transferring knowledge from older to younger workers.

Some organizations have tried to separate generations from working together on assignments, but of these, 78 percent said that this method did not work (Burke 2004). In addition, it is cumbersome to apply.

Millennials can be motivated; they just need to be understood by the other generations. They have been referred to as the self-esteem generation. Ninety percent of Millennials say that they are "happy, confident and positive" (Howe and Strauss 2001). Their independence is grounded in self-promotion (Paine 2006), which may be why employers view them as "entitled" (Alsop 2008). Workers from this generation believe they can afford to be picky, especially with the brain drain of Boomers retiring (Alsop 2008). While there may be some truth to this belief, the challenge is to help younger workers understand that this entitlement mindset may cause them problems in the workforce when interacting with older workers.

Alsop (2008) found that Millennials have high expectations, for instance, an attitude of "What are you going to give me?" They need flexible work routines, and want lots of attention and guidance—constant feedback, but in a caring, gentle way (like their parents gave them). They are not loyal to their companies, but are highly opinionated and fearless. They are the children of the Baby Boomers and Generation X in the workplace. Later Boomer moms gave up their careers for them; Gen X moms wanted their children to have a more secure childhood than they had. The message for older workers is: the younger workers are their kids!

To keep millennials, who are direct reports, engaged, I assign one or two (but no more) tangible (not conceptual) projects or tasks that are sequential, and have pretty linear critical paths, from objective to end deliverable. And projects/tasks that can be delivered in a matter of weeks, not months. I monitor progress every few days (or every day, if needed)—once-weekly check-ins aren't sufficient. When millennials hit road-blocks (i.e., can't get past step 3 in, say, a 10-step process), they tend not to "manage up" particularly well. "I've tried for the last few days to get this report to run, but it still won't" is something I heard recently from a direct report. I had advised spending half a day in discovery; instead, the individual—too self directed and overly confident (or scared)—never made an attempt to check-in, or seek further counsel to arrive at a successful outcome. (Heskett 2007)

There are also gender differences in the Millennial workforce; or rather, there are fewer differences. In the Families and Work Institute's *National Study of the Changing Workforce* (2008), it was found that Millennial women were just as likely as Millennial men to want greater responsibility at work. Millennials were also less interested overall in wanting more responsibility. In 1992, 80 percent of men and 72 percent of women wanted jobs with greater responsibility. By 2008, the desire for more responsibility had dropped to 67 percent for men and 66 percent for women. This is a major shift in the mindset of workers. If additional responsibility is not valued as much as it was fifteen years ago, a new approach is needed to tap into what motivates Millennials.

According to a survey conducted in 2008 of U.S. and Canadian leaders by Birkman and Stanton Chase, only about half (55 percent) of respondents felt that CEOs were willing or very willing to do what was necessary to win the war for talent, although 44 percent recognized the retirement time bomb as a challenge. Seventy-one percent regarded retaining valued employees as a challenge. One way to attract and retain talent is called employer branding. This is the perceived value of working at the organization, and is the basis for competing for talent.

In their book *Generations at Work,* authors Zemke, Raines and Filipczak (2000) say that there are two keys to all the generations working successfully together: "aggressive communication and difference deployment." Aggressive communication means that differences do not get swept under the rug but are talked about openly and resolved. Difference deployment means that generational differences are celebrated and used to the advantage of the company. Zemke et al. describe their approach as the "ACORN Imperative: Accommodate employee differences, Create workplace choices, Operate from a sophisticated management style, Respect competence and initiative, and Nourish retention."

MAXIMIZING INTERGENERATIONAL PERFORMANCE: TRAINING

Sensitivity training in broad generational differences can help minimize potential conflict and maximize collaboration (Harris 2007). Training for older employees to learn how to manage groups that are generationally diverse is particularly helpful. It's important to emphasize similarities as well as differences. In a benchmarking study conducted by Boston College, twenty-five organizations that were considered on the leading edge of managing age diversity were surveyed. Seventy-five percent of them offer supervisory training for managers to help them deal with the intergenerational workforce (Pitt-Catsouphes 2007). The key to this training is intergenerational respect. Accomplishments should be recognized at all career stages. When there are differences in work attitudes based on career stage, generational cohort, or both, these differences need to be treated with respect.

Managers who supervise an age-diverse workforce in particular need to be trained to effectively supervise workers who may have different needs. For example, younger workers tend to want more feedback, but prefer feedback in the form of coaching rather than criticism, no matter how constructive it may be (Fraone n.d.).

One way to help build awareness and sensitivity is to have workshops run by external consultants where age-diverse groups take a personality inventory such as the Myers-Briggs Type Indicator (MBTI) and compare the results. Discussing a personality instrument can help employees on a team realize that there are some personality characteristics that transcend age. For example, MBTI theory postulates that people perceive data in two different ways, either through their five senses or through their intuition. People who use sensing for data gathering tend to be detail-oriented, while people who use intuition for data gathering tend to see the big picture. People also make decisions in two different ways. People who use logic and objective thinking tend to be critical and analytical; people who consider the impact on other people of their actions tend to be more people-oriented. Looking at these differences and seeing that they don't depend on age can help the generations see that there may be more similarities between them than differences.

General Mills uses a board game to help managers and work groups understand and cope with generational differences (Fraone n.d.). Called "Leading through the Generations," it helps to get workers and managers talking about possible differences. Again, the key is to respect differences while recognizing that there are similarities, and avoid making assumptions based on stereotypes.

Linda Duxbury studies the generations in the workforce and has come up with a couple of useful analogies for understanding the differences between the perspectives of various generations that could be useful in a training exercise (as cited in Foster 2006). The first exercise is getting on the bus and the second is the frog in the boiling water.

The bus analogy helps Boomers understand the perspective of younger generations who are waiting to move up in the organization. Early Boomers go to the front of the room and sit in the best chairs. These seats represent the best jobs. Then the later Boomers come along and they get seats that are not as good, but they still get seats. Then younger generations try to catch the bus, but they can't get a seat. They go to a number of different buses because they are only standing, so one particular bus doesn't mean more than another—they are still standing no matter which bus they are on. This helps older generations understand why younger generations may not be as loyal to their organization.

This exercise leads to the next analogy. Conditions on the bus get worse and worse, because there are more people who want to ride the bus than there are seats. The condition of the bus is analogous to the increasingly heavy workload that current workers are struggling with, but are used to as in the old fable about the boiling frog. If you put a frog in water and slowly turn up the heat, it will stay in there until it dies. So Boomers are staying in the workforce even while workloads are getting heavier and heavier. They are used to it. Along come the young frogs (Millennials), and when they jump in the pot, they jump right back out. They recognize that the water is boiling, while the older frogs in the boiling water (Boomers) don't realize it.

The Boomers are critical of the Millennials who jump back out. The young frogs wonder why the older frogs don't jump out of the boiling water, too. The perceptions of each are colored by their expectations of what work is supposed to be like. This analogy can then lead to a general discussion about work norms and new ways to work together without being critical of the other generations.

Here's the perspective of one Millennial (Heskett 2007):

> I, as a Millennial, grew with stories of lay-offs to people 6 months from receiving pensions, underfunded retirement plans, corporate greed at employee expense, immoral and unethical political representatives and the total fallacy that is Social Security for my generation. You will have to forgive me if I do not feel inclined to "pay my dues" only to have my gold watch reneged. We are not cynical (for the most part) about these systemic issues. Indeed quite the opposite, we are hopeful in some respects and are eager to take the reins for ourselves, which is construed by some as overzealousness.

Paine (2006) offered the following strategies for dealing with the intergenerational workforce. While all employees need to feel connected to the mission of the organization and to the achievement of organizational results, younger generations are always reevaluating their organizational significance and need to know what their contribution is. If they do not see a contribution, then they may likely leave for another organization where they can feel that they are making a contribution. On the other hand, older generations do not need to know as much about their particular contribution to where the organization is headed; they likely had an influence in developing the strategic goals and took for granted that their accomplishments were in line with them.

Direct communication is extremely important as well. While older generations depend on formal communication via the performance appraisal, younger generations demand honest, specific, direct, and relevant feedback on their performance. They also want to be able to give such feedback to their managers.

Leadership development will be critical due to the retirement skills gap. Younger generations need to be trained, mentored, and enabled to obtain networks. Since younger generations expect to have many growth opportunities that are not necessarily part of a traditional career path, providing multiple, flexible career paths is essential. This is particularly important as Generation X waits for its turn leading organizations. Additionally, Millennials need a broad range of experiences to prepare them for the leadership positions that will be left vacant after older workers retire and Generation X has moved up. Opportunities for leadership development will also help attract and retain younger workers, as they want to have as much responsibility and learn as much as they can. The organizations that can offer this kind of flexible career routing and development will be more likely to win the war for talent.

Similar to implementing FWA in the last chapter, organizations need to focus on outcomes-based rather than time-based management. Veterans were heavily influenced by military styles of accomplishment, so they are very task-oriented. In contrast, Boomers are process-oriented. Gen X wants to get the job done as soon as possible, and doesn't want to be told how to do it, just what the overall objective is. They want to figure out the rest on their own, due to their independent nature. Millennials also want to do this, but they need more coaching and supervision than Gen X. Millennials will want to know clearly what is expected and what the deadlines are.

All generations want access to training and development opportunities, but preferences for learning delivery are different between older and younger workers. Older workers expect formal classes with lectures and little interaction and participation. This may not be the best way to learn, but this has been the way organizations have done it. Younger generations want customized training, preferably online and with on-demand access. They don't want to wait until a class is scheduled; they want to learn at their own pace and at a time of their choosing. Even so, researchers are finding that Millennials still require some formal training, especially in being a part of a virtual team (Charsky, Kish, Briskin, Hathaway, Walsh and Barajas 2009). The authors suggest that younger workers may view technology more as a way to interact socially than as a way to get work done.

Finally, Paine (2006) suggests creating a flexible work environment to retain younger generations. As we saw in Chapter 5, the desire for flexibility is something that is common across the generations. The perception may be that only the younger workers want flexibility, but when this notion is looked at more carefully, perhaps in a workshop, the desire for flexibility is more widespread. While younger generations like the Millennials may not yet have families, they want the extra time to volunteer or to have as much autonomy as possible. Gen X and younger Boomers have families and want flexibility to be able to more easily balance their work and nonwork lives. Eldercare and childcare is important to them as well. Finally, we have seen in Chapter 5 that flexibility is a key requirement for older Boomers looking to cut back their hours or to delay retirement. An awareness of this common need for flexibility, although for different reasons can help the generations see that there are commonalities.

MITRE Corporation has conducted what they call Networking Circles (Fraone n.d.) They hold luncheons every month that are facilitated by two employees, each from different generations. They discuss both technical and personnel topics such as career development. The circles were formed after focus groups held by the company determined that networking for professional and social purposes was needed. This illustrates the importance of asking your employees what they feel is needed to communicate with each other better.

MAXIMIZING INTERGENERATIONAL PERFORMANCE: TEAM BUILDING

One area where all this age diversity and generational conflict can cause problems is when working on a team (Macon and Artley 2009). Challenges are also opportunities for growth and higher performance. Diversity on teams adds to performance because different perspectives can be shared and blind spots are minimized. The availability of teams made up of multiple generations actually enhances knowledge sharing in organizations (Slagter 2009).

According to Patrick Lencioni (2002), author of *The Five Dysfunctions of a Team*, there are five barriers to effective teams: lack of trust, avoiding conflict, not being committed, not wanting to be accountable, and not paying attention to results. How will generational differences affect possible team dysfunctions? Certainly younger and older workers may regard each other without trust since they do not understand each other well. Intergenerational sensitivity training would be a good idea before working in a team, but this isn't always feasible.

Building trust requires time. Trust building as described in the last chapter would be useful here as well. Lencioni (2002) notes these five ways to build trust: sharing history, discussing contributions and barriers for each individual team member, using personality inventories, using 360 feedback to provide constructive criticism, and experiential exercises.

Sharing history can be particularly effective for multigenerational groups. Younger workers may not have a good understanding of the work history of older workers. They may not even want to hear it! However, if younger worker are encouraged in a spirit of team building to not only share their perspectives but listen to the perspectives of others on the team, it could be very beneficial to team performance. Older workers also need to listen to the perspectives of younger workers. Perhaps the sharing could even be done in a fun atmosphere, which would make it easier for younger workers to participate. General Mills' game could also be useful here as a team-building exercise.

Another model useful for intergenerational teams is Tuckman's (1965) group process model. In the first phase, *forming*, group members are polite with each other. The next stage, *storming*, is when conflicts begin to surface and be dealt with openly within the group. This is where some intergenerational stereotypes may come into play. Younger workers are usually more comfortable on teams than older ones. Younger workers have been put on teams since they were in school. They will want to participate right away and get going. Older workers may be slower and want to discuss process and roles. Next is the *norming* phase, when the team members develop rules about how they should interact with each other. Putting norms in place about things group members may have conflict about, such as working hours, helps the team develop into a performing team.

Slagter (2009) suggests that teams made up of different generations can facilitate awareness of generational differences and similarities. Groups can be asked questions such as "What is teamwork?" and "How should we cooperate and work together?" Like sharing histories, answering these kinds of questions can help each generation understand the other better.

Focusing on commonalities between all age cohorts may be more useful than focusing on differences. Smith (2008) wrote that all employees want to be respected, recognized, and remembered (3 R's) and coached, consulted, and connected (3 C's). The trick is to help each of the generations see past some superficial differences to more enduring commonalities.

Fine (2009) offered these tips for intergenerational teams: Respect is paramount and requires behaviors and attitudes that signal the importance of the contribution of each generational member. Stereotypes about how much can be expected from people due to their age need to be avoided. Assumptions about how workers want to work based on their generation should also be avoided. Differences should be openly discussed when they interfere with team effectiveness. Get to know each member of the team. Don't assume that performance issues have to do with age or generations.

CAN WE ALL GET ALONG?

The important thing for older workers to remember is that they taught their children to expect more from their environment, particularly parents of Millennials. Now their children are in the workforce, expecting the management and supervision that they got from their parents. This is what Veterans and Boomers would have wanted from the workplace as well—older generations just never demanded it before. Millennials know that organizations need them, and they are willing to walk away and start their own companies to compete with the companies that couldn't attract or retain them. In attempting to attract and retain younger workers, organizations will also attract and retain older workers who might otherwise retire earlier and create the skills shortage. This results in a win-win for employers and employees alike.

> Whatever you want to call the next generation, remember, they are our kids. We raised them! I really get tired of people harping on this generation. I am proud of my children and hope they keep the energy and perspective they have. We need them to keep improving life for everyone. They will not put up with some of the things we did. Great! Possibly that is why some of the CEOs are having trouble. This generation will not put up with talk and no action. I have also seen them walk out the door of a job when they feel they have been treated unfairly. They will test accountability. It is not just a word for them. (Heskett 2007)

Millennials themselves don't see a problem with older workers retiring. Here's what one Millennial manager had to say (Heskett 2007):

> We are in an age of specialization, and the rules have changed. The greatest change I see is in hiring and retention. Businesses which are not adapting, and remain married to the process of blindly searching for degrees and certifications, and who judge employee reliability based on "time served" at other companies are failing to attract, hire, or retain the high knowledge workers. They are top heavy on authoritarians who treat employees like children, and they are going to suffer the most in change management as retirement hits. And, then they'll come-a-calling. There may currently be a resistance to turning executive roles over to my generation, but the reality is we are the ones best suited to weather and/or foster the imminent and necessary change which results from the mass retirement of the Baby Boomers.

Ready or not, the younger generation feels ready to take over the reins from retiring Boomers.

CHAPTER 7

Retirement or Continued Engagement

The traditional view of retirement, which serves as the basis of most of the retirement systems in the United States, is based on the traditional stages of life, or a standard life cycle of humans. These stages are: *birth to beginning education* (age 0–6), *education* (age 6 to 18 or 21), *work* (age 18 or 21 to 65) and *retirement and old age* (age 65 plus). Also, until the last half of the twentieth century, the time span for being retired was relatively short. Life expectancy in the United States at the beginning of the twentieth century was age 47, but by the end of the century it had reached 77. For those who were age 65 in 2001, the remaining life expectancy for men was 16.4 years and for women was 19.4 years (U.S. Department of Health and Human Services 2001). These data suggest a need for a reevaluation of what men and women will do with their life in what Shoshana Zuboff (2004) has termed "the new adulthood."

The trend since the decade of the 1970s, particularly for men, has been to retire at increasingly younger ages, but there is evidence that this trend may be leveling off and perhaps reversing. According to an analysis done by the U.S. Department of Labor (Toossi 2004), the labor force participation rate for both men and women age fifty-five and over shifted from a decline of 2.3 percentage points between 1982 and 1992 to increases in participation of 4.9 points between 1992 and 2002, with a projected increase of 5.1 points between 2002 and 2012. The participation rate for men age fifty-five and over declined by 5.4 points between 1982 and 1992, but increased by 3.2 points between 1992 and 2002 and is projected to increase by 3.8 percentage points between 2002 and 2012. The labor force participation by women age fifty-five and over has continued to increase from the growth of 0.1 percentage points between 1982 and 1992 to 5.9 points between 1992 and 2002 and is projected to increase to 6.0 points between 2002 and 2012.

According to the results of a 2008 survey by Sun Life Financial discussed by John D'Antona in the publication *Workforce Week* (2009), only 48 percent of American workers plan to retire at age sixty-seven. The other 52 percent said they plan to work longer. The data from the survey also showed that only 46 percent of those surveyed are "very confident" they will have enough money to take care of basic living expenses at sixty-seven, and 28 percent are "very confident" they will be able to take care of medical expenses. Younger generations have little confidence that government benefit programs such as Social Security and Medicare will be available when they retire, as 63 percent of workers aged 30–39 don't believe Social Security will be available. The same age group also noted the need for employer-sponsored health-care benefits as a reason to work past sixty-seven.

A Roper Starch study for AARP (1999), found considerably higher optimism for working after retirement than the Sun Life Financial study. Roper Starch found that 87 percent of the Baby Boomers planned to continue to work in retirement, either by choice or necessity. As acknowledged in the study, however, actual behavior of the Baby Boomers as they approach retirement age and eligibility may not match their responses on prospective behavior.

In a paper prepared by Sara Rix (2001) for the Japan Institute of Labor Millennium Project, she noted that the trend toward working longer in the United States has been increasing slowly but steadily since the mid-1990s. She cited six reasons for this trend:

- Workers may not be financially prepared to retire at age 62 (the earliest age at which one can receive Social Security retirement benefits) or at age 65 (the age for full social security retirement benefits, which is slowly rising to age 67)
- Employer-provoked pension coverage has leveled off since the 1970s to about half the wage and salary workforce
- Among those workers covered by private pension plans, the proportion of *defined contribution* plans has risen sharply at the

expense of *defined benefit* plans (see the discussion below describing these types of retirement plans)

- Many workers live from paycheck to paycheck and have little in the way of retirement savings
- Rising life expectancy is raising concerns among workers with savings that they might outlive those savings, and/or they wonder how they will fill their time during a long period of retirement
- Educational levels are higher among the Baby Boomers, who are increasingly the prospective retirees, and higher educational levels are associated with a greater probability of postponing retirement

Many of the beliefs about how and when workers should and will retire are based on the social construct of "traditional" retirement: workers leaving paid work and living the balance of their lives in the state of retirement and leisure (Atchley and Barusch 2004; Auerbach and Welsh 1994). This concept of life proceeding in regular stages follows from the work of Erikson (1997). However, more recent studies of how people actually behave reflect that work and retirement follows a more irregular *life cycle* pattern (Atchley and Barusch 2004; Marshall and Mueller 2002). Han and Moen (1999) also found that retirement followed a temporal historical pattern of historical context, social heterogeneity, and biographical pacing related to generational cohort, gender, and career pathway factors.

Based on the pioneering work on the *life cycle* of people by Erikson and others (Erikson 1997; Erikson, Erikson and Kivnick 1986), some researchers have begun considering a flexible and more iterative "life course" approach (Atchley and Barusch 2004; Dychtwald 1999; Marshall and Mueller 2002) or one based on "critical life events" (Diehl 1999) for studying aging and retirement issues. In this view, retirement and work are seen as becoming more cyclical than linear. Therefore, future studies of incentives which drive the decision of older workers to stay or leave or return to the workplace would be better developed in relation to this life-course perspective.

Rocco, Stein and Lee (2003) also argue that the traditional retirement-to-old-age phase of life is now shifting to a *third age* in which ". . . the workspace becomes a dynamic space for older workers," work ". . . becomes a search for continued meaning and contribution as well as to satisfy a financial need," and ". . . older workers might make the decision to remain in, retire from or return to periods of part-time, full-time or seasonal or holiday work" (p. 156).

THE CONTEXT OF RETIREMENT

Retirement can be viewed from three levels: (1) the individual retiree, (2) the organization from which they retired, and (3) the society as a whole (Beehr and Bennett 2007). From the workers' point of view, retirement is usually viewed with anticipation for some form of leisure funded by benefits they believe they have earned for long service in the workforce. From the organizational perspective, especially as the workforce ages and life span increases, obligations for paying benefits to retirees for a long period of time become more and more burdensome. From a society perspective, the payment of benefits from taxpayer-funded programs such as Social Security and Medicare are becoming a concern as well. This latter concern is often voiced in some manner of intergenerational transfer (passing the cost on to our children) and the steady decline in the number of active workers supporting retirees. We will briefly discuss each of these perspectives in turn.

The Individual Retiree Perspective

Is Retirement Passé?

At the turn of the twentieth century, through their human resource organizations and in cooperation with labor unions, companies sought to ensure some stability in the labor market and loyalty from employees through various employee benefit programs such as pensions. The federal government added to this form of welfare capitalism with the establishment of the Social Security system at the start of the Great Depression. Additionally, changes in federal tax rules incentivized companies to offer more fringe benefits, such as pensions, than wage increases to their employees. The idea behind these programs was a sort of risk sharing where employers gained additional control over their workforces and employees gained greater job security and insurance against life risks (Shuey and O'Rand 2004).

Is the Shift in Risk-sharing in Retirement Plans between Employers and Employees a Cause for Rethinking Retirement?

At the turn of the twenty-first century, all risk-sharing bets seemed to be off the table. Risk sharing among employees (through union or group pension investment and health insurance programs) and between employers and employees is shifting to most or all the risk being shouldered by employees. Much of this risk shift in pension plans occurred during the last two decades of the twentieth century. Information from the Employee Benefit Research Institute (2002) and a study by Verma and Lichtenstein (2003) shows that, in addition to Social Security, over half of U.S. workers have participated in some type of private or public sector pension plan during their working careers. Also, three-fourths of workers over age fifty-five have some type of pension coverage beyond Social Security. These private sector and public pension plans are generally of two broad types: *defined benefit* and *defined contribution* plans.

Overall, the percentage of men who participated in an employer-offered retirement plan declined from 97 percent to 81 percent between 1979 and 1999. For women, the decline was from 93 percent to 74 percent. During this same period, the number of employees covered by defined contribution plans more than doubled while those employees under defined benefit plans dropped by almost 15 percent during the same period (U.S. Department of Labor 2002 as cited in Shuey and O'Rand 2004). It is expected that this trend will continue and probably accelerate as those in defined benefit retirement plans begin to retire.

Among all workers, participation in defined benefit plans has fallen from 32 percent in 1993 to 20 percent in 2007, while participation in defined contribution plans has risen from 35 percent to 43 percent during the same period (Bureau of Labor Statistics 2009, March). In defined benefit plans, companies promise to pay workers a specified amount in retirement benefits. In defined contribution plans, companies promise to contribute a specified amount, but make no assurance as to the final payout. Among all workers, there has been a decrease in the percentage covered by defined benefit (*payout*) plans and an increase in the percentage covered by defined contribution (*pay in*) plans. For more and more workers, this means that risk—in terms of steady retirement income—has been transferred from the employer to the eventual retiree.

Defined Benefit Retirement Plans

From the perspective of the worker, defined benefit plans have been favored; some employees actively sought positions with employers who provided plans of this type (Penner, Perun and Steuerle 2002). These plans in the past provided a relatively predictable and stable annuity based on a combination of average pay (for example, over the last three to five years of employment), length of service in the organization, and age at retirement. In recent years, the low-risk aspect of these pension plans has become questionable (see our discussion below on the crisis in pension plans in the airline and automotive industries in recent years). These plans are usually set up to pay a fixed monthly amount to an eligible employee during their retirement years. Contributions by both the employee and the employer are based on actuarial projections of age at death minus age at retirement to determine the amount of the required contribution to the retirement fund during working years. Generally there is a ceiling on the amount of contribution. Most private organizational plans of this type specify a minimum retirement age of sixty-five or a combination of age and years of service (e.g., total of eighty-five) to receive a full annuity. Some plans also allow for an earlier retirement with a reduced payout. Most plans of this type are mandatory for employees of the organization and are fully managed by the employer either directly or through an independent fund manager.

Defined Contribution Retirement Plans

Defined contribution plans have a potential for larger or smaller benefits than defined benefit plans, with more risk of variability in retirement benefits falling on the worker. Because of the often lower long-term cost and liability to them, U.S. employers are increasingly shifting to these types of plans (Schulz 2001). Under these types of plans, the amount the employee receives at retirement is not fixed in advance, but is based on the level of contribution by the employee, such as with a 401(k) plan, or with some matching by the employer. The amount in the employee's account is based on the return on investment of the funds in the account. This investment is often in mutual funds, company stock, a profit-sharing arrangement, or other investment combinations. These investments in these plans are usually self-directed through the fund manager who was selected by the employer or a union or other employee association. For the employee, these plans have more risk and potential reward than defined benefit plans. In most cases defined contribution plans are voluntary and provide pension portability for workers who change organizations frequently. These types of plans usually favor younger workers who have more time to plan and select investment opportunities that provide retirement benefits in the future (Penner, Perun and Steuerle 2002).

Because there is more risk placed on employees in defined contribution retirement plans, there is more incentive for them to delay retirement based on growing returns or to await an increase in returns after a market downturn such as the one experienced in 2000–2001, and more dramatically in 2008–2009. Thus organizations may also be encouraging older workers to stay in the workforce longer by accelerating the trend of shifting retirement plans from the defined benefit type to the defined contribution type. On the other hand, if returns from the stock market and other investments again accelerate as they did in the late 1990s, older workers may retire in greater numbers.

THE SHIFTING CONCEPT OF RETIRING

Aside from the increased financial risks encumbering workers who are considering retirement, the idea of *retirement* itself as a terminal event (exit from work to leisure) may be a dying concept. It is generally thought that as a worker approaches the normal retirement age of sixty-five he or she begins to lose focus on the job and focus more on looking forward to the leisure of retirement. However, this view is not supported by most research in the area. As Robert Atchley and Amanda Barusch (2004) note in their summary of findings on attitudes toward work and retirement

> People can be positive about both work and retirement at the same time. The value placed on having meaningful, fulfilling and enriching work changes very little with age. (pp. 247–248)

They found that attitudes are generally favorable toward retirement regardless of the worker's gender. However, they also found that whether or not workers anticipated a happy retirement at age sixty-five varied significantly with their expected financial security. They noted that 80 percent of potential retirees expected at least some financial challenges in retirement. This attitude could be expected to be even bleaker in today's recessionary environment.

Not all workers who reach the normal retirement age of sixty-five wish to retire or actually do so, and their motivation to continue working may or may not be primarily related to economic need. Parnes and Sommers (1994), for example, studied data from the National Longitudinal Surveys of Older Men to examine the most important characteristics that related to continued employment of men into their seventies and eighties. The characteristics with the most significant correlations to continued employment were good health, a strong psychological commitment to work, and a corresponding distaste for retirement. The probability of continued employment by these men was also found to be positively related to their higher level of educational attainment and being married to a working wife, but was negatively related to the level of income in the absence of work.

Increasingly, the decision about when to retire and whether or not employees will be able to retire at the same age and rate as their predecessors is being overtaken by events outside their control.

Adequacy of Income and Other Assets for Retirement

The availability of Social Security, pensions and assets for retirement income, continued health benefits after retirement, and family obligations (such as child- and eldercare) have been areas suggested as some of the personal influences on the decision to retire by older workers (Atchley and Barusch 2004; Dailey 1998; Mitchell and Fields 1984; Rocco, Stein and Lee 2003). The relationship between rising income levels and the level of continued participation in the workforce by older workers is also a factor in the decision to retire. In general, workers can more easily retire if they believe that income in retirement will be adequate to support the lifestyle desired (Clark, York and Anker 1999) and/or they do not see that working longer will provide increased income sufficient to offset additional years of deferred benefits (Penner, Perun and Steuerle 2002). The results of a study by Costa (1998), however, revealed that in recent years income has been less and less a factor in the retirement decision, as retirees' relative wealth has increased along with their ability to migrate to lower-cost areas upon retirement.

Shifts in the Context of Retirement

The pattern of retirement at age 62–65 in the United States has been a relatively recent phenomenon, which began during the economic depression of the 1930s. One action taken, in order to reduce the high unemployment during the depression, was the creation of the Social Security system in 1935. The idea behind Social Security was to provide a retirement program for older Americans to encourage them to leave the workplace and make way for younger workers. After the economy recovered from the depression, and especially after the end of World War II, companies also began providing private pension plans that further encouraged retirement by older workers.

The psychological and economic aspects of retirement are the usual focus of most studies of retirement. However, even if older workers desire to stay in the workforce past traditional retirement age, there are social norms, public policies, and organizational factors that may deter or prevent them from remaining. The social and cultural context of the retirement process, how it impacts the decision to retire, and how successful one is at adapting to retirement have only had limited investigation by researchers (Luborsky 1994). In addition, health status and the need to provide care for a family member may not allow older workers to remain in the workforce (Atchley and Barusch 2004). Furthermore, the nonmonetary benefits of continuing to work versus retiring have increasingly come to the fore. In a recent article in *U.S. News and World Report*, Emily Brandon (2009) cited ten reasons why a person should not retire based on recent research. A few pertinent nonmonetary reasons she cited were that seniors who continue to work, even on a part-time basis, seem to enjoy better health; their marriages were less negatively impacted; their lives had more meaning; and their social life was better.

Baby Boomer Retirement May Differ from That of Predecessor Generations

The Baby Boomers, in particular, may not want to move into traditional retirement as a life of leisure without working (Montenegro, Fisher and Remez 2002). However, given that the Baby Boomer generational cohort spans nineteen birth years and represents a broad segment of American society, it is difficult if not impossible to make generalizations about the cohort in terms of income, lifestyle, beliefs and values, or potential retirement behavior. Jeffrey Zaslow (2004) makes this point clearly in a *Wall Street Journal* article:

> There is a great distance between Barry Manilow and Barry Bonds. Mr. Manilow, the singer, was born in the first year of the postwar baby boom. About 76 million births later, Mr. Bonds, the baseball slugger, became one of America's last baby boomers. That was in 1964, when demographers say the boom ended. (D-1)

One recent effort to focus on potential retirement behavior of Baby Boomers was the study by Roper Starch (1999) for AARP. The Roper Starch study was based on segmented sets of shared values and was conducted in five phases. The first phase was a review of Roper Starch databases and prior studies on demographic and economic characteristics of Baby Boomers. Phase two was a qualitative study using eight focus groups of Baby Boomers in the four cities of Chicago, Illinois; Providence, Rhode Island; Charlotte, North Carolina; and Phoenix, Arizona. The third phase was a quantitative survey conducted by thirty-minute telephone interviews of 2,001 randomly selected Baby Boomers from among the U.S. population aged 35–52 in 1999. In phase four, the survey data were segmented by respondent attitudes, beliefs, and behaviors regarding retirement.

The fifth and final phase involved a postsurvey interview with eight focus groups based on the segment types from the segment analysis in two cities, Chicago and Baltimore. The segmentation analysis in phase four resulted in a clustering of five segments. In order of percentage of the total sample, these segments were the *self-reliants* (30 percent), *traditionalists* (25 percent), *anxious* (23 percent), *enthusiasts* (13 percent), and *strugglers* (9 percent).

The self-reliants were currently putting money into various savings and investment vehicles that they were fairly sure they could count on as sources of retirement income. They also planned to work part-time in retirement, mainly for interest or enjoyment.

The traditionalists were strongly confident that both Social Security and Medicare would be available to them when they retired. In addition, they said they planned to continue to work at some level in retirement.

The anxious, as the name suggests, were not optimistic about retirement. Their annual income fell about $10,000 below the average of all Baby Boomers in the sample. They were particularly concerned that they were not putting enough money aside for retirement and that they would have inadequate health-care insurance coverage in retirement. Most of them believe that they will not be able to quit working in their retirement years.

The enthusiasts, on the other hand, cannot wait to retire. All of them felt that they would have plenty of money and they did not plan to work in their retirement. They envisioned a retirement focused on recreation and leisure.

The strugglers, whose annual income was about $30,000 below the Baby Boomer average, recognize that they were not putting enough money aside for retirement, but felt that they could not do so given their current financial needs. Compared to the other groups, they reported not having given much thought to retirement. This latter group was also disproportionately comprised of females (64 percent).

Based on the Roper Starch analysis, 87 percent of the Baby Boomers planned to continue to work in retirement, either by choice or necessity. As acknowledged in the study, however, actual behavior of the Baby Boomers as they approach retirement age and eligibility may not match their responses on prospective behavior. For example, in the survey 39 percent of the sample Baby Boomers agreed with the statement "I can't imagine myself retired," but 44 percent disagreed. The study also cites prior Roper Starch research which indicates that as workers get closer to retirement, the more comfortable they become with the idea of retirement.

Baby Boomer Women and Retirement

The major limitation of the 1994 Parnes and Sommers study, and virtually all studies of retirees until more recently, is that it included only the perspectives of men. Part of the reason for this limitation is that, until the last fifteen years, relatively few women had worked sufficiently long enough in a career or for an organization to gain retirement benefits and were, thus, largely tied to the benefits accumulated by a spouse for retirement (Dailey 1998). In addition, women generally have a different attitude than men toward work and retirement. As noted by Choo (1999),

> In contrast with the sudden and often traumatic break older men make with employment, older women prefer to remain at work provided they can balance the competing demands of family and personal expectations. This can be provided by providing flexible work options such as phased retirement and part-time work. (p. 71)

Some recent studies are initiating the dialogue about whether or not Baby Boomer women in particular, despite their significant penetration into the full-time labor market, are at a disadvantage for future retirement vis-à-vis Baby Boomer men (Calasanti and Slevin 2001; Dailey 1998). Calasanti and Slevin (2001), for example, found that Baby Boomer women would be disadvantaged in retirement income because of social inequalities between men and women and the male-biased structure of both private pension and Social Security systems. These studies also show that social expectations for family care roles and differing labor market participation patterns than men will likely result in Baby Boomer women, especially those who have less education and are single minorities, being at risk of not being financially secure in retirement. Other studies have dealt with particular behavioral aspects surrounding decisions by women to completely or partially retire (Honig 1985), how the marital status of women impacts the retirement decision (Szinovacz and DeViney 2000) and gender influences on workers' goals for retirement (Hershey, Jacobs-Lawson and Neukam 2002).

Retirement benefits for women also often are at a lower level than for men because women have generally earned lower lifetime earnings than men. There is continuing disagreement about whether these lower lifetime earnings are the result of occupational segregation of women into more routine and less complex jobs that are considered "women's work," which have lower pay scales (Simpson, Greller and Stroh 2002), or if their lower pay is the result of a gendered labor process and lower access to training (Tomaskovic-Devey and Skaggs 2002), or a combination of these factors. Also, women who have not worked full time for a full career or who have not been employed outside the home are partially or fully dependent on receiving a portion of the benefits or survivor benefits based on the income of their spouses. If they are divorced, unless provided by a court in a divorce settlement, they are cut off from this source of retirement income. Also, even if not divorced, some of their spouses' retirement benefits may not pass to them upon the death of their spouse or they may be passed on at a reduced level.

However, such studies of women facing retirement, particularly those from the Baby Boomer generation, are still limited. Also, most retirement programs that exist in the United States, and most studies of retirees and retirement, are still premised on the norm of the male family breadwinner working in a long-term career job and then retiring on a pension determined by a combination of age and years of service to a single company, despite evidence that that model of retirement is fast disappearing (Dailey 1998; Schulz 2001).

THE ORGANIZATIONAL PERSPECTIVE

Pension plans and their increasing costs have been a major concern by large organizations and have come to the fore as a national concern during the past decade. The automobile industry and the airline industry in the United States have been particularly hard hit as their unfunded liabilities in their pension programs were in the multibillions of dollars. As part of the bailout relief provided by the federal government (after September 11, 2001 for the airlines and since 2007 for the automotive industry), the retirement benefits for several of the largest of these pension plans were allowed by the government to be substantially reduced and shifted from their generous defined benefit model to a much less generous defined contribution model for employees retiring in the future.

There is much controversy and finger-pointing on the cause of the meltdown of these larger pension systems. Most observers, however, lay part of the blame for this occurrence at the feet of the leadership of the organizations themselves and part at the feet of the employees and their representatives. During the heyday of the automobile industry, labor unions continued to propose, and company leaders accepted, increasingly generous pay, benefits, and retirement benefits. The companies were making very good profits and the employees shared in the bounty. Economists, business analysts, and public policy leaders continue to wrangle over the causes, but it is clear that both the industry leaders and the employees and their unions were not paying attention to the effects of the aging workforce, increasing automation of manufacturing, foreign competition, the recessionary economy, and other environmental factors that were making their pension systems untenable.

Provision of Continued Health-care Insurance Coverage in Retirement

The availability of reasonably priced health insurance after retirement, at least for a long enough period to bridge the gap until Medicare is available at age sixty-five, is also a factor in the decision of workers to retire or stay in the workplace. A cross section of older workers and retirees questioned on the importance of continued affordable health insurance for a recent study for the AARP and information from a report by the Organisation for Economic Co-operation and Development (OECD) supported this view (Montenegro, Fisher and Remez 2002; OECD 2001). The affordability of health insurance is a growing factor for most organizations with the significant rise in health-care costs over the past few years.

Until recently, many organizations provided continued health insurance for retirees on the same basis as active employees. However, because of the rising costs, more organizations are increasingly moving away from providing health insurance coverage for retirees. The cost of retiree health insurance plans are largely driving this shift, as has been seen dramatically in the recent financial crises affecting the automotive and airline industries in the U.S.

Bridge Employment or Phased Retirement

The United States leads many countries in the number of people involved in some form of bridge employment between their long-term careers and full retirement (Taylor 2002). However, most of these arrangements seem to be self-directed by the employee and not part of a formal employer system. In addition, many of these arrangements are based on a shift to lower-paying jobs from those the senior worker had during his or her career which may make them less motivated to continue to contribute at a high level (Rix 2001). The formalization of bridge employment or gradual retirement has also been limited by the structure of many government and private retirement plans, and the potential conflict with existing laws and regulations affecting senior workers and retirees (Penner, Perun and Steuerle 2002; Rix 2001). Employers, to date, have not moved in large numbers toward providing formal bridge employment opportunities. Part of the reason for this has been a lack of an overall strategy for retaining senior workers on at least a part-time basis; however, there are some legal and structural impediments to establishing bridge retirement programs as well.

The formalization of bridge employment or phased retirement has been limited by the structure of many government and private retirement plans and the potential conflict with existing laws and regulations affecting older workers and retirees (Penner, Perun and Steuerle 2002). Additionally, where formal bridge retirement or gradual retirement programs have been formalized in other countries, such as Finland and Japan, the impact on retaining older workers and reducing ageism in the workplace has had limited success (Taylor 2002).

Phased retirement could take a number of forms (Hedge, Bormann and Lammlein 2006). Some of the more common forms are:

- Reducing work hours gradually
- Granting employees leaves of absence to try retirement to see if it works for them
- Permitting senior workers to engage in some form of job-sharing arrangement to allow for reduced work hours
- Keeping retirees on as consultants, part-time, temporary, or seasonal workers

Daniel Feldman (1994) analyzed the individual worker's decision to retire early or move to retirement through *bridge employment*, based on four factors, each with several dimensions. The four factors are "individual differences," "opportunity structures in the career path," "organizational factors," and the "external environment." Individual differences include *work history, marital status, demographic status* (gender and race), *health status, attitudes toward work,* and *attitudes toward retirement.* Opportunity structures in the career path include *age-related performance decrements* (physical, intellectual, social), *discrimination against older workers, type of industry,* and the *primary versus the secondary job market.* Organizational factors include *financial rewards* (wages and pensions), *early retirement counseling programs,* and *flexibility in managing older workers.*

Table 7.1
Workers' Decision to Retire Early or Move to Bridge Employment

Individual differences	Opportunity structures in the career path	Organizational factors	External environment
• Work history • Marital status • Demographic status (gender & race) • Health status • Attitudes toward work • Attitudes toward retirement	• Age related performance decrements (physical, intellectual, social) • Discrimination against older workers • Type of industry • Primary versus secondary job market	• Financial rewards (wages & pensions) • Early retirement counseling programs • Flexibility in managing older workers	• Uncertainty about macroeconomic trends • Social Security eligibility and laws • Economic growth • Government programs to assist older workers

Source: Feldman, 1994.

The external environment includes the *uncertainty about macroeconomic trends, social security eligibility and laws, economic growth,* and *government programs* (see Table 7.1).

Feldman focused on the worker's decision to retire early, accept bridge employment in his or her current occupation and industry or others, and his or her perceived ability to adjust satisfactorily to retirement:

- *Workers who are more likely to retire early.* These workers have the positive aspects of remaining with an organization longer, being married and having spouses who also work, being in primary labor market jobs versus secondary labor market jobs, having higher current wages and expected future pension benefits, receiving comprehensive preretirement counseling, working for an organization that is flexible in managing older workers, having higher certainty about macroeconomic trends (such as continued relatively high interest rates and stock market growth which enhance their retirement assets and income), and having certainty about plans for retirement. On the negative side, these workers work for large firms in declining manufacturing industries, face discrimination based on age, gender, or race, have major physical illnesses and functional impairments, and experience greater negative impact of age on performance.

- *Workers who are more likely to accept bridge employment in their current occupation and industry.* These workers are those who have the positive aspects of working for organizations that have high flexibility in managing older workers and do not discriminate based on age, gender, or race, and having higher certainty about macroeconomic trends. On the other hand, these workers are more likely to have higher current wages and expected future pension benefits, psychosomatic versus physical illnesses, greater negative impact on performance due to age, and have a self-identity that is tied to the organization.

A later study of bridge employment decisions by older workers by Weckerle and Shultz (1999) further supports Feldman's analysis.

The results of these two studies provide fruitful information for organizational leaders in developing workforce policies vis-à-vis older workers with a view toward retaining those they wish to keep engaged, either full time or through bridge employment, while encouraging others to retire from the organization.

Legal and Government Policy Impediments to Employer-provided Retirement Flexibility

There are several impediments to the development and implementation of phased or flexible retirement plans for employers in the United States. According to a study by the Employment Policy Foundation in 2003 (as noted in Dychtwald, Erickson and Morison 2006, p. 57), 65 percent of U.S. employers would like to offer flexible retirement arrangements but feel that they are blocked from doing so by regulatory restrictions. Three sets of regulations cover pension and benefits:

- ERISA: the Employment Retirement Income Security Act. This act imposes rules on the uniformity of treatment of employees and their pension benefits which inhibit employers from making special arrangements for their most skilled and valued employees;
- IRS: the U.S. Internal Revenue Service. IRS regulations prohibit defined-benefit retirement plans from making distributions to an employee until his or her employment ends or he or she reaches

"normal retirement age." Coupled with a provision in ERISA, the IRS code can even prohibit distribution after normal retirement age in some situations. Other tax laws can impose penalties on employees (before age fifty-nine and a half) for the withdrawal of funds from their 401(k) and similar retirement saving plans. These laws also restrict an employee's ability to manage sources of income during deceleration toward, or phased, retirement;

• ADEA: the Age Discrimination in Employment Act. ADEA requires equal benefits, such as health insurance, regardless of age. This 1967 law also defines *older worker* as one over forty years of age. This can cut both ways. For example, if a sixty-year-old receives preferred treatment, a forty-year-old can protest.

Dychtwald and his colleagues (2006) note that some workarounds have been developed to partially overcome some of these restrictions:

• Reducing hours worked for an employee moving toward retirement. This is often done by continuing the person's pension contribution but paying no benefits. The risk is that under most defined-benefit plans, the employee's retirement pay is based on some average pay formula over the last few years of employment.

• Implementing a retiree-return program, hiring retirees as contractors. The restriction here is that they cannot work more than 1,000 hours per year unless they are clearly "independent consultants."

• Engaging retirees as independent consultants.

• Inviting employees to continue to work under some other revised arrangement. Not everyone would be in favor of this, and employers in some cases might have to adjust their customary or mandatory retirement ages.

Flexible Retirement versus Phased Retirement

Ken Dychtwald and his colleagues (Dychtwald, Erickson and Morison 2006) argue that organizations employing *phased retirement* approaches are focusing in the wrong direction. They point out that phased retirement is just a slowdown of the process of getting senior workers out the door. They argue instead for *flex retirement*:

Flexible retirement means not only *partial retirement*, so that employees can enjoy other pursuits, but also *active retirement*, wherein employees remain productively and socially engaged in the workplace. It means *ongoing work*, often starting before retirement age and continuing decades later, and not shedding employees to reduce costs. (p. 52)

Through this approach, they note that employers can achieve several important business goals, such as:

- Retaining the services of key employees and top performers
- Retaining and transferring industry, project, and customer knowledge and expertise
- Providing highly experienced temporary talent pools to accommodate fluctuations in staffing needs
- Retaining leadership talent to fill unexpected gaps
- Controlling unit cost of labor by getting the same skilled labor but saving the cost of benefits

MAINTAINING A RELATIONSHIP WITH RETIRED ALUMNI

Some organizations have kept a cadre of retired employees in an advisory or consultant role, on either a full- or part-time basis. Most of those who have been offered this role have specific hard-to-find or hard-to-train skills (such as insurance actuaries) or have been in key leadership positions and can provide advice on strategy and direction for the organization. To date, these efforts have been limited and sporadic across organizations.

Often there is no formal program for such consultant or advisor arrangements. Even where a formal program exists, it is far from predictable from employees' perspectives, and thus does not allow them to incorporate the program into their retirement planning.

As noted above in the discussion of phased retirement, laws and regulations still exist in the United States that can make it difficult if not impossible for organizations to offer phased retirement to employees, especially on a selective basis. These include questions about how to assure conformance to the provisions of the ADEA, ERISA, and IRS rules (see the discussion above), such as how does an employer retain those employees it wants to keep and not those it does not; how to assure that employed alumni are really retired.

RETIREMENT PLANNING FOR THOSE WHO MUST LEAVE

Most retirement planning programs offered by organizations are based on how to handle financial issues in retirement, an explanation of what benefits continue and which do not (such as health insurance), and what type of annuity or retirement income will be provided from their retirement plan. Unfortunately, few retirement planning programs help retirees deal with the more transcendental challenges and opportunities retirement can bring. Dealing with the question of what they are to do with the rest of their lives is one of those challenges and opportunities.

The Meaning of Retirement: What to Do with the Rest of Your Life

During the early years of work life, people typically either become engaged with the work itself or the organization they are in and its values and goals, or they fall into the daily grind of getting the job done in exchange for salary and promotion. Either track can sustain them for some period of time, particularly when also facing the challenges of supporting a family or meeting other needs external to the workplace. It is usually when they reach midcareer and midlife that they start to look both backward and forward and reflect on what they have accomplished, what their values are, and what they want to do in the future.

Increasingly, if they have the opportunity and wherewithal, they seek a new job, career, or other life direction. We see this phenomenon among younger workers who shift jobs and careers at a greater rate than their Baby Boomer and older colleagues (at least this was true until the current recession).

The Baby Boomers on the other hand have generally become more loyal to their organizations and more stable in their careers as they have aged and have stayed put. However, they are now reaching a crossroad as they approach the traditional retirement age. For some, this can be a difficult time as their identity and much of the meaning in their lives may be so tied to their jobs and career that facing retirement generates the same sense of loss as the death of a loved one. As Po Bronson noted in an article in the magazine *Fast Company* 2003 (Bronson 2003), they are reaching the point where they have both the opportunity and the challenge of asking and acting upon the question "What should I do with my life?" As the Baby Boomers approach retirement they could become immobilized and afraid both of asking the question and of the answer. Organizations should design their retirement planning programs to help them find the answer. This may result in benefits if the answer is that they would like to stay engaged in some form with the organization (see the discussion of maintaining a relationship with retired workers, above, and Chapter 4 on bringing them back).

CONCLUSION

Retirement has been seen as a terminal event in one's life or, at best, a transition from work to leisure. The concept of retirement has shifted especially among the Baby Boomers who are approaching the traditional retirement age of sixty-five. Many of them are saying that they want to continue to be engaged in some form of meaningful work and they want to be valued for their contribution. Hopefully, this is good news for organizations that are facing considerable brain drain from the potential loss of some of their most valued and experienced workers, managers, and leaders from the Baby Boomer cohort. The challenge is to accommodate this shift in attitude toward retirement and provide a workplace which is welcoming to the Boomers and reflects their value to the organization. It is our hope that this book will provide some insight into both the problem and the solution.

References

Ahlrichs, Nancy S. 2007. Managing the generations differently to improve performance and profitability. *Employee Relations Today* 34 (1): 21–31.

Allen, Steven G. 2001. Technology and the wage structure. *Journal of Labor Economics* 19 (2): 440–83.

Alsop, Ron. 2008. *The trophy kids grow up: How the millennial generation is shaking up the workplace.* San Francisco: Jossey-Bass.

Anderson, Stella E., Betty S. Coffey, and Robin T. Byerly. 2002. Formal organizational initiatives and informal workplace practices: Links to work-family conflict and job related outcomes. *Journal of Management* 28 (6): 787–811.

Atchley, Robert C., and Amanda S. Barusch. 2004. *Social forces and aging: An introduction to social gerontology,* 10th ed. Belmont, CA: Wadsworth/Thomson Learning.

Auerbach, James A., and Joyce C. Welsh. 1994. *Aging and competition: Rebuilding the U.S. workforce.* Washington, DC: National Planning Association.

Bailyn, Lotte. 1993. *Breaking the mold: Women, men, and time in the new corporate world.* New York: Free Press.

Barnes-Farrell, Janet L., and Russell A. Matthews. 2007. Age and work attitudes. In *Aging and work in the 21st century,* eds. Kenneth S. Shultz and Gary A. Adams. Mahwah, NJ: Lawrence Erlbaum Associates.

Barrah, Jamie L., Boris Baltes, Kenneth S. Shultz, and Heidi E. Stolz. 2004. Men's and women's eldercare-based work-family conflict: Antecedents and work-related outcomes. *Fathering* 2 (3): 305–30.

Barth, Michael C., William McNaught, and Philip Rizzi. 1996. The costs and benefits of older workers. In *Handbook on employment and the elderly*, ed. William Crown. Westport, CT: Greenwood Press.

Beales, Sylvia. 2000. We should invest in older women and men: The experience of Help Age International. *Gender and Development* 8 (2): 9–18.

Becker, Gary. 1993. *Human capital: With special reference to education*, 3rd ed. New York: Columbia Univ. Press.

Beehr, Terry A., and Misty M. Bennett. 2007. Examining retirement from a multilevel perspective. In *Aging and work in the 21st century*, eds. Kenneth S. Shultz and Gary A. Adams. Mahwah, NJ: Lawrence Erlbaum Associates.

Bernard, Miriam, and Judith E. Phillips. 2007. Working careers of older adults. *Community, Work and Family* 10 (2): 139–60.

Besl, John R., and Balkrishna D. Kale. 1996. Older workers in the 21st century: Active and educated, a case study. *Monthly Labor Review* 119 (6): 18–28.

Birkman and Stanton Chase. 2008. Business implications of the new reality 2008. How the war for talent is impacting organizations throughout North America and what to do about it, http://www.stantonchase.com/best_practices/Business_Implications_New_Reality.pdf.

Blair-Loy, Mary, and Amy S. Wharton. 2002. Employees' use of work-family policies and the workplace social context. *Social Forces* 80 (3): 813–45.

Block, Peter. 1993. *Stewardship: Choosing service over self-interest*. San Francisco: Berrett-Koehler.

Bongaarts, John. 2004. Population aging and the rising cost of public pensions. *Population and Development Review* 30 (1): 1–23.

Bowers, Philip H. 2001. Is retirement sustainable? In *Ageism in work and employment*, eds. Ian Glover and Mohamed Branine, 97–114. Aldershot, UK: Ashgate.

Bowman, Kaye, and Peter Kearns. 2007. E-learning for the mature age worker. http://pre2009.flexiblelearning.net.au/flx/webdav/site/flxsite/shared/Research%20and%20Policy%20Advice/Report_Mature_Aged_Workers.pdf.

Brandon, Emily. 2009. 10 reasons you shouldn't retire: Your 401(k), social life, and even your health could benefit from a few more years in the workforce. *U.S. News and World Report*.

Bronson, Po. 2003. What should I do with the rest of my life: The real meaning of success—and how to find it. *Fast Company* 66: 69–79.

Bruce, Willa, and Christine Reed. 1994. Preparing supervisors for the future workforce—the dual-income couple and the work-family dichotomy. *Public Administration Review* 54 (1): 36–43.

Buahene, Adwoa and Giselle Kovary. 2007. The great divide. *HR Professional* 24 (5): 2–30.

Buhler, Patricia M. 2008. Are you prepared for the talent shortage? *Supervision* 69 (7): July.

Bureau of Labor Statistics. 2008, October. Older workers: Are there older people in the workforce? Washington, DC: U.S. Bureau of Labor Statistics.

————. 2009, March. Defined-contribution plans more common than defined-benefit plans. *Program perspectives: On Retirement benefits* 3. Washington, DC: U.S. Bureau of Labor Statistics.

————. 2009, December. *Employment status of the civilian noninstitutional population by age, sex, and race, Table A-13*. Washington, DC: U.S. Bureau of Labor statistics. http://www.bls.gov/web/cpseea13.pdf (accessed January 13, 2010).

Burggraf, Shirley P. 1998. *The feminine economy and the economic man: Reviving the role of family in the post-industrial age*. Cambridge, MA: Perseus Books.

Burke, Mary E. 2004. Generational differences survey report. Alexandria, VA: SHRM Research.

Burtless, Gary, and Joseph F. Quinn. 2002. Is working longer the answer for an aging workforce? *An Issue in Brief* 11. Boston: Trustees of Boston College, Center for Retirement Research.

Butrica, Barbara A., and Cori I. Uccello. 2004. *How will boomers fare at retirement?* Washington, DC: AARP.

Calasanti, Toni M., and Kathleen F. Slevin. 2001. *Gender, social inequality and aging*. Walnut Creek, CA: AltaMira Press.

Callanan, Gerald A. and Jeffrey H. Greenhaus. 2008. The baby boom generation and career management: A call to action. *Advances in Developing Human Resources* 10 (1): 70–85.

Calo, Thomas J. 2007. Boomer generativity: An organizational resource. *Public Personnel Management* 36 (4): 387–95.

Cameron, Kim S., and Robert E. Quinn. 2006. *Diagnosing and changing organizational culture: Based on the competing values framework*, rev. ed. San Francisco: Jossey-Bass.

Card, Laura, and Mark O'Donnell. 2004. Ejection vs. retention: Weighing the pros and cons of employing elders. http://www.bsad.uvm.edu/files/aging/chapter2.pdf.

Casey, Patrick R., and Joseph G. Grzywacz. 2008. Employee health and well-being: The role of flexibility and work-family balance. *Psychologist-Manager Journal* 11 (1): 31–47.

Challenger, John A. 2003. The coming labor shortage. *Futurist* 37 (5): 24–28.

Charness, Neil, Sara Czaja, and Joseph Sharit. 2007. Age and technology for work. In *Aging and work in the 21st century*, eds. Kenneth S. Shultz and Gary A. Adams. Mahwah, NJ: Lawrence Erlbaum Associates.

Charsky, Dennis, Mary L. Kish, Jessica Briskin, Sarah Hathaway, Kira Walsh, and Nicolas Barajas. 2009. Using communication technology to facilitate teamwork. *TechTrends* 53 (6): 42–48.

Choo, Teh Eng. 1999. The aging workforce: Some implications, strategies and policy considerations for human resource managers. *Asia Pacific Journal of Human Resources* 37 (2): 37–60.

Clark, Robert L., E. Anne York, and Richard Anker. 1999. Economic development and labor force participation of older persons. *Population Research and Policy Review* 18: 411–32.

Cleveland, Jeanette N., and Lynn Shore. 1992. Self and supervisory perspectives on age and work attitudes and performance. *Journal of Applied Psychology* 77: 469–84.

Collison, Jessica. 2003. *Older workers survey*. Alexandria, VA: Society for Human Research Management.

Costa, Dora L. 1998. The evolution of retirement: Summary of a research project. Papers of the hundred and tenth annual meeting of the American Economic Association. *Journal of Economic Review* 88-2: 232–236.

Costello, Cynthia. 1997. *Training older workers for the future, changing work in America series*. Cambridge, MA: Radcliffe Public Policy Institute.

Covey, Stephen M. R. 2006. *The speed of trust*. New York: Free Press.

Cummings, Thomas G., and Christopher G. Worley. 2005. *Organization development and change*, 8th ed. Marion, OH: South-Western.

Czaja, Sara J. 2001. Technological change and the older worker. In *Handbook of psychology of aging*, eds. James E. Birren and K. Warner Schaie, 547–68. Academic Press.

Dailey, Nancy. 1998. *When baby boom women retire*. Westport, CT: Praeger.

D'Antona, John D. 2009. 48 percent of U.S. workers target age 67 for retirement. *Workforce Week:* October.

Delong, David W. 2004. *Lost knowledge*. New York: Oxford Univ. Press.

Dess, Gregory G., and Jason D. Shaw. 2001. Voluntary turnover, social capital, and organizational performance. *Academy of Management Review* 26: 446–56.

den Dulk, Laura, and Judith de Ruijter. 2008. Managing work/life policies: Disruption vs. dependency arguments. Explaining managerial attitudes towards employee utilization of work-life policies. *International Journal of Human Resources Management* 19 (7): 1222–36.

de Valk, Peter. 2003. Ageing workforce issue now a matter of extreme urgency. *Personnel Today:* 20–22.

Diehl, Manfred. 1999. Self-development in adulthood and aging: The role of critical life events. In *The self and society in aging processes*, eds. Carol Ryff and Victor W. Marshall, 150–83. New York: Springer.

Dychtwald, Ken. 1999. *Age power: How the 21st century will be ruled by the new old*. New York: Tarcher/Putnam.

Dychtwald, Ken, Tamara Erickson, and Bob Morison. 2004. It's time to retire retirement. *Harvard Business Review* 82 (3): 48–57.

Dychtwald, Ken, Bob Morison, and Tamara Erickson. 2006. *Workforce crisis: How to beat the coming shortage of skills and talent.* Boston: Harvard Business School Press.

Employee Benefit Research Institute. 2004. *Retirement confidence survey, 2004: Retirement confidence fact sheet.* Washington, DC: Employee Benefit Research Institute, American Savings Education Council and Mathew Greenwald & Associates.

Erikson, Erik H. 1997. *The life cycle completed.* New York: Norton.

Erikson, Erik H., Joan M. Erikson, and Helen Q. Kivnick. 1986. *Vital involvement in old age.* New York: Norton.

Even, William E., and David A. Macpherson. 1994. Gender differences in pensions. *Journal of Human Resources, Special Issue: Women's Work, Wages and Well-Being* 29-2: 555–87.

Eversole, Barbara A. W. 2005. Understanding differential organizational responses to work/family issues: The role of beliefs, attitudes, and decision making styles of chief executive officers. PhD diss., Colorado State Univ.

Eversole, Barbara A. W., Gene Gloeckner, and James H. Banning. 2007. Understanding differential organizational responses to work/family issues: The role of beliefs and decision-making styles of chief executive officers. *Journal of European and Industrial Training* 31 (4/5): 259–73.

Feldman, Daniel C. 1994. The decision to retire early: A review and conceptualization. *Academy of Management Review* 19 (2): 285–311.

———. 2007. Career mobility and career stability. In *Aging and work in the 21st century*, eds. Kenneth S. Shultz and Gary A. Adams. Mahwah, NJ: Lawrence Erlbaum Associates.

Finley, Michael E., and James O. Bennett. 2002. Safety and the blue collar worker: Are older workers considered in program development? *Professional Safety* May: 34–38.

Fine, Ben, and Francis Green. 2000. Economics, social capital, and the colonization of the social sciences. In *Social capital: Critical perspectives*, eds. Stephen Baron, John Field, and Tom Schuller, 78–93. New York: Oxford Univ. Press.

Fine, Jo Renee. 2009. Improving intergenerational teams. http://www.shrm.org/hrdisciplines/Diversity/Articles/Pages/ImprovingIntergenerationalTeams.aspx.

Fossum, John A., Richard D. Arvey, Carol A. Paradise, and Nancy E. Robbins. 1986. Modeling the skills obsolescence process: A psychological/economic integration. *Academy of Management Review* 11: 362–74.

Foster, Kris. 2006. Mind the GAP. http://magazine.carleton.ca/2006_Spring/1733.htm.

Franklin, Mary Beth. 2007. I flunked retirement. Twice. *Kiplinger's Personal Finance* 61 (7): 68–71.

Fraone, Jennifer S., Danielle Hartmann, Kristin McNally. (n.d.). The multigenerational workforce: Management implications and strategies for collaboration. Boston College Center for Work and Family, Executive Briefing Series. http://www.bc.edu/centers/cwf/research/publications/meta-elements/pdf/MultiGen_EBS.pdf.

Freedman, Marc. 1999. *Prime time: How baby boomers will revolutionize retirement and transform America.* Cambridge, MA: Perseus Books.

Friedland, Robert B., and Laura S. Summer. 1999. *Demography is not destiny.* Washington, DC: National Academy on an Aging Society.

Friedman, Stewart D. and Jeffrey H. Greenhaus. 2000. *Work and family—Allies or enemies?* New York: Oxford University Press.

Galunic, D. Charles, and Erin Anderson. 2000. From security to mobility: Generalized investments in human capital and agent commitment. *Organization Science* 11 (1): 1–20.

Geroy, Gary D., and Donald L. Venneberg. 2003. A view to human capital metrics. In *Critical issues in HRD: An agenda for the twenty-first century,* eds. Ann M. Gilley, Jamie L. Callahan, and Laura L. Bierema, 87–103. Cambridge, MA: Perseus Books.

Geroy, Gary D., Amber Bray, and Donald L. Venneberg. 2005. The CCM model: A management approach to performance optimization. *Performance Improvement Quarterly* 18 (2): 22–39.

Godshalk, Veronica M., and John J. Sosik. 2000. Does mentor-protégé agreement on mentor leadership behavior influence the quality of a mentoring relationship? *Group & Organization Management* 25: 291–317.

Goldberg, Beverly. 2000. *Age works: What corporate America must do to survive the graying of the workforce.* New York: Free Press.

Gordon, Edward E. 2005. *The 2010 meltdown: Solving the impending jobs crisis.* Westport, CT: Praeger.

Grzywacz, Joseph, Dawn Carlson, and Sandee Shulkin. 2008. Schedule flexibility and stress: Linking formal flexible arrangements and perceived flexibility to employee health. *Community, Work and Family* 11 (2): 199–214.

Gustman, Alan L., and Thomas L. Steinmeier. 2000. Retirement in dual-career families: A structural model. *Journal of Labor Economics* 18 (3): 503–45.

Han, Shin-Kap, and Phyllis Moen. 1999. Clocking-out: Temporal patterning of retirement. *American Journal of Sociology* 105 (1): 191–236.

Harper, Sarah, Hafiz Kahn, Atulyah Saxena, and George Leeson. 2006. Attitudes and practices of employers towards ageing workers: Evidence from a global survey on the future of retirement. *Ageing Horizons* 5: 31–41.

Harris, Paul. 2007. Flexible work policies mean business. *Training & Development* 61 (4): 32–36.

Hedge, Jerry W., Walter C. Borman, and Steven E. Lammlein. 2006. *The aging workforce: Realities, myths, and implications for organizations.* Washington, DC: American Psychological Association.

Hegewisch, Ariane, and Janet C. Gornick. 2008. *Statutory routes to workplace flexibility in cross-national perspective.* Washington, DC: Institute for Women's Policy Research.

Herman, Roger E., Tom G. Olivo, and Joyce L. Gioia. 2003. *Impending crisis: Too many jobs too few people.* Winchester, VA: Oakhill Press.

Hershey, Douglas A., Joy M. Jacobs-Lawson, and Kirstan A. Neukam. 2002. Influences of age and gender on workers' goals for retirement. *International Journal of Aging and Development* 55 (2): 163–79.

Heskett, Jim. 2007. How will millennials manage? http://hbswk.hbs.edu/5736.html.

Hill, Jeffrey E., Andre'a D. Jackson, and Giuseppe Martinengo. 2006. Twenty years of work and family at International Business Machines, *American Behavioral Scientist* 49 (9): 1165–1183.

Home Depot. 2004. *http://storecareers.homedepot.com/aarp.* Downloaded July 22, 2004.

Honig, Marjorie. 1985. Partial retirement among women. *Journal of Human Resources* 20 (4): 613–21.

Horning, Karl H., Anette Gerhard, and Matthias Michailow. 1995. *Time pioneers: Flexible working time and new lifestyles.* Cambridge, MA: Blackwell.

Howe, Neil and William Strauss. 2000. *Millennials rising.* New York: Random House.

Huber, Gregory A., and Thomas J. Espenshade. 1997. Neo-isolationism, balanced budgets and the fiscal impacts of immigrants. *Population Migration Review, Special Issue: Immigrant Adaptation and Native Born Responses in the Making of Americans* 31 (4): 1031–54.

Ilmarinen, Juhani. 2003. Promotion of work ability during aging. In *Aging and work,* ed. Masaharu Kumashiro, 21–35. New York: Taylor & Francis.

Imel, Susan. 1991. Older worker training: An overview. *ERIC Digest* 114. Columbus, OH: ERIC Clearinghouse Center on Education and Training for Employment.

James, Jacquelyn B., Jennifer E. Swanberg, and Sharon P. McKechnie. 2007. Responsive workplaces for older workers: Job quality, flexibility and employee engagement. *Issue Brief* 11. Boston: The Center for Aging and Work at Boston College.

Johnson, Arlene, Karen Noble, and Amy Richman. 2005. Business impacts of flexibility: An imperative for expansion. Corporate Voices for Working

Families. http://www.cvworkingfamilies.org/publication-toolkits/business
-impacts-flexibility-imperative-expansion-november-2005.

Johnson, Harold E. 1997. *Mentoring: For exceptional performance.* Glendale,
CA: Griffin.

Johnson, James A., and John Lopes. 2008. The intergenerational workforce,
revisited. *Organizational Development Journal* 26 (1): 31–36.

Johnson, Richard W., and David Neumark. 1997. Age discrimination, job sep-
arations and employment status of older workers: Evidence from self-
reports. *Journal of Human Resources* 32 (4): 113–29.

Johnson, Stephanie K., Gary D. Geroy, and Orlando V. Griego. 1999. The
mentoring model theory: Dimensions in mentoring protocols. *Career
Development International*: 384–91.

Kaihla, Paul. 2003. The coming job boom. *Business 2.0*, 4-8: 97–105.

Kaplan-Leiserson, Eva. 2001. Aged to perfection. *Training & Development* 55: 16.

Karoly, Lynn A., and Jeannette A. Rogowski. 1994. The effect of access to
post-retirement health insurance on the decision to retire early. *Industrial and Labor Relations Review* 48 (1): 103–23.

Kelly, Erin L., Eric C. Dahlin, Donna Spencer, and Phyllis Moen. 2008. Making sense of a mess: Phased retirement policies and practices in the
United States. *Journal of Workplace Behavioral Health* 23 (1/2): 147–64.

Kelly, Erin L., Ellen E. Kossek, Leslie B. Hammer, Mary Durham, Jeremy Bray,
Kelly Chermack, Lauren A. Murphy, and Dan Kaskubar. 2008. Getting
there from here: Research on the effects of work-family initiatives on
work-family conflict and business outcomes. *Academy of Management
Annals* 2 (1): 305–49.

Knowledge@Wharton. 2005. Older workers: Untapped assets for creating
value. http://knowledge.wharton.upenn.edu/article.cfm?articleid=1123.

———. 2007. Workplace loyalties change, but the value of mentoring doesn't.
http://knowledge.wharton.upenn.edu/article.cfm?articleid=1736.

Knowles, Malcolm. 1973. *The adult learner: A neglected species.* Houston: Gulf.

Kochan, Thomas, Wanda Orlikowski, and Joel Cutcher-Gershenfeld. 2002.
Beyond McGregor's theory y: Human capital and knowledge-based
work in the 21st century organization. Paper presented at the Sloan
School 50th Anniversary Session, October 11, in Cambridge, MA.

Koc-Menard, Sergio. 2009. Flexible work options for older workers. *Strategic
HR Review* 8 (2): 31–36.

Kofodimos, Joan. 1995. *Beyond work-family programs: Confronting and resolving
the underlying causes of work-personal life conflict.* Greensboro, NC:
Center for Creative Leadership.

Koppes, Laura L. 2008. Facilitating an organization to embrace a work-life
effectiveness culture: A practical approach. *Psychologist-Manager Journal*
11: 163–84.

Kossek, Ellen E., and Mary D. Lee. 2008. Implementing A reduced-workload arrangement to retain high talent: a case study. *Psychologist-Manager Journal* 11: 49–65.

Laabs, Jennifer J. 1998. They want more support—inside and outside of work. *Workforce* 77 (11): 54–56.

Lambrechts, Frank, and Hilda Martens. 2008. The reemployment process of older managers after a plant closing: Towards a career transition framework. *Business Renaissance Quarterly* 3 (1): 41–75.

Lancaster, Lynne C., and David Stillman. 2002. *When generations collide: Who they are, why they clash, how to solve the generational puzzle at work.* New York: HarperCollins.

Lencioni, Patrick. 2002. *The five dysfunctions of a team.* San Francisco: Jossey-Bass.

Lerman, Robert I., and Stefanie R. Schmidt. 2003. *An overview of economic, social and demographic trends affecting the U.S. labor market.* Washington, DC: Urban Institute.

Levin-Epstein, Jodie. 2006. Getting punched: the job and family clock. Center for Law and Social Policy, http://www.clasp.org/admin/site/publications/files/0303.pdf.

Luborsky, Mark R. 1994. The retirement process: Making the person and cultural meanings malleable. *Medical Anthropology Quarterly*, New Series 8, 4: 411–429.

Mackavey, Maria G. and Richard J. Levin. 1998. *Shared purpose: Working together to build strong families and high-performance companies.* New York: AMACOM.

Macon, Max, and James B. Artley. 2009. Can't we all just get along? A review of the challenges and opportunities in a multigenerational workforce. *International Journal of Business Research* 9 (6): 90–94.

Madrian, Brigitte C., Gary Burtless, and Jonathan Gruber. 1994. The effect of health insurance on retirement. *Brookings Papers on Economic Activity* 1: 181–252.

Magid, Renee Yablans. 1990. *The work and family challenge: No ordinary employees . . . no ordinary managers.* New York: American Management Association.

Marshall, Victor W., and Margaret M. Mueller. 2002. Rethinking social policy for an aging workforce and society: Insights from the life course perspective, *CPRN Discussion Paper* W18. Ottawa, ON: Canadian Policy Research Networks.

McEvoy, Glenn M., and Mary Jo Blahna. 2001. Engagement or disengagement? Older workers and the looming labor shortage. *Business Horizons* 44: 46.

McHugh, Kevin E. 2003. Three faces of ageism: Society, image and place. *Ageing and Society* 23: 165–85.

McLean, Mike. 2008. Flexibility in the workplace. *Journal of Business: Spokane* 23 (12): 21. http://findarticles.com/p/articles/mi_qa5289/is_20080529/ ai_n26683940/.

Montenegro, Xenia, Linda Fisher, and Shereen Remez. 2002. *Staying ahead of the curve: The AARP work and career study conducted for AARP by Roper ASW.* Washington, DC: AARP.

Moore, Maggie C., and Nancy R. Lockwood. 2007. Work/life balance series part II: Work/life balance: A global perspective. http://www.from shrm.org.

Moseley, James L., and Joan C. Dessinger. 2007. *Training older workers and learners: Maximizing the performance of an aging workforce.* San Francisco: Pfeiffer.

Nemanick, Richard C. Jr. 2000. Comparing formal and informal mentors: Does type make a difference? *Academy of Management Executive* 14: 136–38.

Neumark, David, and Wendy A. Stock. 1999. Age discrimination laws and labor market efficiency. *Journal of Political Economy* 107 (5): 1081–1125.

OECD. 2001. The well-being of nations: The role of human and social capital countries. Paris: Organisation for Economic Co-operation and Development.

Ohman, Kathleen A. 2000. Critical care managers change views, change lives. *Nursing Management* 9: 32B–32E.

Older Workers Treated Differently: Findings of a Conference Board Survey of HR Executives. 2003. *Work & Family Newsbrief* 6.

O'Sullivan, S. O. 2003. Great jobs: Our annual hot list. *AARP the Magazine* 20 (11): 51–55.

Overman, Stephanie. 1999. Make family-friendly initiatives fly. *HR Focus* 76 (7): 14–15.

Paine, Jill W. 2006. Cross-generational issues in organizations. Sloan Work and Family Research Network. http://wfnetwork.bc.edu/encyclopedia _entry.php?id=4156&area=All.

Parnes, Herbert S., and David G. Sommers. 1994. Shunning retirement: Work experience of men in their seventies and eighties. *Journal of Gerontology: Social Sciences* 49 (3): S117–24.

Parsloe, Eric, and Monika Wray. 2000. *Coaching and mentoring: Practical methods to improve learning.* Sterling, VA: Stylus.

Penner, Rudolph G., Pamela Perun, and Eugene Steuerle. 2002. *Legal and institutional impediments to partial retirement and part-time work by older workers.* Washington, DC: Urban Institute. http://www.urban.org/publications/ 410587.html.

Peterson, Peter G. 2004. *Running on empty: How the democratic and republican parties are bankrupting our future and what Americans can do about it.* New York: Farrar, Straus and Giroux.

Peterson, Suzanne J., and Barry K. Spiker. 2005. Establishing the positive contributory value of older workers: A positive psychology perspective. *Organizational Dynamics* 34 (2): 153–67.

Phillips, Jean M., Mary Pomerantz, and Stanley M. Gully. 2007. Plugging the boomer drain: Can your organization stay afloat during the talent crisis? Here are challenges and solutions to consider as baby boomers jump ship. *HR Magazine* 52 (12): 54–58.

Piktialis, Diane. 2007. Adaptations to an aging workforce: Innovative responses by the corporate sector. *Generations* 31 (1): 76–82.

Pitt-Catsouphes, Marcie. 2007. Between a twentieth- and a twenty-first-century workforce: Employers at the tipping point. *Generations* 31 (1): 50–56.

Pitt-Catsouphes, Marcie, and Christina Matz-Costa. 2008. The multi-generational workforce: Workplace flexibility and engagement. *Community, Work & Family* 11 (2): 215–29.

Rafter, Michelle V. 2008. Phased retirement: Firms wing it. *Workforce Management* 87 (2): 27–31.

Rapoport, Rhona, Lotte Bailyn, Joyce K. Fletcher, and Bettye H. Pruitt. 2002. *Beyond work-family balance.* San Francisco: Jossey Bass.

Rhebergen, Bertien, and Ida Wognum. 1997. Supporting the career development of older employees: An HRD study in a Dutch company. *International Journal of Training and Development* 1: 191–98.

Richman, Amy L., Janet T. Civian, Laurie L. Shannon, Edward Jeffrey Hill, and Robert T. Brennan. 2008. The relationship of perceived flexibility, supportive work-life policies, and use of formal flexible arrangements and occasional flexibility to employee engagement and expected retention. *Community, Work & Family* 11 (2): 183–97.

Rix, Sara E. 2001. Restructuring work in an aging America: What role for public policy? In *Restructuring work and the life course,* eds. Victor W. Marshall, Walter R. Heinz, Helga Kruger, and Anil Verma, 72–89. Toronto: Univ. of Toronto Press.

Rix, Sara E. 2001. Toward active ageing in the 21st century: Working longer in the United States. Paper presented for the Japanese Institute of Labour Millennium Project, November 2001, in Tokyo, Japan.

Rocco, Tonette S., David Stein, and Chan Lee. 2003. An exploratory examination of the literature on age and HRD policy development. *Human Resource Development Review* 2 (2): 155–80.

Roper Starch Worldwide. 1999. *Baby Boomers envision their retirement: An AARP segmentation analysis.* Washington, DC: AARP.

Ross, Catherine E., and Patricia Drentea. 1998. Consequences of retirement activities for distress and the sense of personal control. *Journal of Health and Social Behavior* 39: 317–34.

Rothwell, William J., Harvey L. Sterns, Diane Spokus, and Joel M. Reaser. 2008. *Working longer: New strategies for managing, training, and retaining older employees.* New York: American Management Association.

Roundtree, Linda, and Karen Kerrigan. 2007. Flex-Options Guide. http://www.we-inc.org.

Rust, John, and Christopher Phelan. 1997. How Social Security and Medicare affect retirement behavior in a world of incomplete markets. *Econometrica* 65 (4): 781–831.

Safi, Asila, and Darrell N. Burrell. 2007. The role of mentoring in succession planning and talent in non-profit and governmental organizations. *International Journal of Business and Management* 2 (5): 167–73.

Salkowitz, Rob. 2008. *Generation blend: Managing across the technology age gap.* Hoboken, NJ: Wiley.

Schein, Edgar H. 2004. *Organizational culture and leadership,* 3rd ed. San Francisco: Jossey-Bass.

Schulz, James H. 2001. *The economics of aging,* 7th ed. Westport, CT: Auburn House.

Seagrave, Kerry. 2001. *Age discrimination by employers.* Jefferson, NC: McFarland.

Shuey, Kim M., and Angela M. O'Rand. 2004. New risks for workers: Pensions, labor markets and gender. *Annual Review of Sociology* 30: 453–77.

Simpson, Patricia A., Martin M. Greller, and Linda K. Stroh. 2002. Variations in human capital investment activity by age. *Journal of Vocational Behavior* 61: 109–38.

Slagter, Floor. 2009. HR practices as predictors for knowledge sharing and innovative behavior: A focus on age. *International Journal of Human Resource Development and Management* 9 (2/3): 223–49.

Smith, David I., and Renee E. Spraggins. 2001. *Gender 2000: Census 2000 brief.* Washington, DC: U.S. Department of Commerce, Economics and Statistics Administration, U.S. Census Bureau.

Smith, W. Stanton. 2008. Decoding generational differences: Fact, fiction, or should we just get back to work? http://www.totalpicture.com/shows/career-connections/decoding-generational-differences.html.

Smola, Karen W., and Charlotte D. Sutton. 2002. Generational differences: Revisiting generational work values for the new millennium. *Journal of Organizational Behavior* 23: 363–82.

Solomon, Charlene M. 1999. Workers want a life! Do managers care? *Workforce* 78 (8): 54–57.

Soonhee, Kim. 2003. Linking employee assessments to succession planning. *Public Personnel Management* 32 (4): 533–47.

Stein, David. 2000. The new meaning of retirement. *ERIC Digest* 217, ED440296. Columbus, OH: ERIC Clearinghouse Center on Education and Training for Employment.

Stein, David, Tonette Rocco, and Kelly Goldenetz. 2000. Age and the university workplace: A case study of remaining, retiring and returning older workers. *Human Resource Development Quarterly* 11 (1): 61–80.

Stern, Scott. 1994. Ability, promotion, and optimal retirement. *Journal of Labor Economics* 12 (1): 119–37.

Szinovacz, Maximiliane E., and Stanley DeViney. 2000. Marital characteristics and retirement decisions. *Research on Aging* 22 (5): 470–98.

Tahmincioglu, Eve. 2007. The quiet revolution: Telecommuting. http://www.msnbc.com/id/20281475/print/1/displaymode/1098/.

Taylor, Mary Ann, and Holly A. Geldhauser. 2007. Low-income older workers. In *Aging and work in the 21st century,* eds. Kenneth S. Shultz and Gary A. Adams. Mahwah, NJ: Lawrence Erlbaum Associates.

Taylor, Philip. 2000. *New policies for older workers.* Bristol, UK: Policy Press, Cambridge Univ.

Thompson, Cynthia A., Laura L. Beauvais, and Karen S. Lyness. 1999. When work-family benefits are not enough: The influence of work-family culture on benefit utilization, organizational attachment, and work-family conflict. *Journal of Vocational Behavior* 54 (3): 392–415.

Tomaskovic-Devey, Donald, and Sheryl Skaggs. 2002. Sex segregation, labor process organization, and gender earnings inequality. *American Journal of Sociology* 108 (1): 102–28.

Toossi, Mitra. 2004. Labor force projections to 2012: The graying of the U.S. workforce. *Monthly Labor Review* 127 (2): 37–57.

Tuckman, Bruce. 1965. Developmental sequence in small groups. *Psychological Bulletin* 63 (6): 384–39.

Twenge, Jean M. 2006. *Generation me.* New York: Free Press.

U.S. Department of Health and Human Services, Center for Disease Control and Prevention, National Center for Health Statistics. 2001. *Health, United States 2003, table 27 Life expectancy at birth, at 65 years of age, and at 75 years of age, according to race and sex: United States, selected years 1900–2001.* http://www.cdc.gov/nchs/data/hus/tables/2003/03hus027.pdf.

Van Deusen, Frederic R., Jacquelyn James, Nadia Gill, and Sharon McKechnie. 2008. Overcoming the implementation gap: How 20 leading companies are making flexibility work. Boston College Center for Work and Family. http://www.bc.edu/centers/cwf/meta-elements/pdf/Flex_ExecutiveSummary_for_web.pdf.

Venneberg, Donald L. 2005. The experience of retirees and their decision to return to the workforce: Implications for organizations. PhD diss., Colorado State Univ.

Vincola, Ann. 1998. Cultural change is the work/life solution. *Workforce* 77 (10): 70–73.

Watkins, Karen E. 1995. Changing managers' defensive reasoning about work/family conflicts. *Journal of Management Development* 14 (2): 77–88.

Watt, Linda. 2004. Mentoring and coaching in the workplace. *Canadian Manager* 29 (3): 14–16.

Xu, Jiaquan, Kenneth D. Kochanek, and Betzaida Tejada-Vera. 2009. Deaths: Preliminary data for 2007. *National Vital Statistics Reports* 58 (1).

Zaslow, Jeffrey. 2004. The latest generation gap: Boomers are often unfairly lumped together. *The Wall Street Journal*, D1.

Zemke, Ron, Claire Raines, and Bob Filipczak. 2000. *Generations at work: Managing the clash of veterans, boomers, xers and nexters in your workplace*. New York: AMACOM.

Zuboff, Shoshana. 2004. The new adulthood. *Fast Company* 85: 92.

Index

Note: Page references followed by "*t*" denote tables.

About the Authors

DONALD L. VENNEBERG, PhD, is an assistant professor in the Organizational Performance and Change Program at Colorado State University. His teaching areas are in workforce development, performance management, and the facilitation of change in organizations. His research and recent publications are in the areas of mentoring and the recruitment, development, and retention of older workers. He was formerly a senior executive with the federal government. His last position was as the deputy chief information officer for the U.S. General Services Administration (GSA), a multibusiness line agency of 14,000 employees. In this and prior executive and management positions, he successfully supervised, trained, and developed people in technical and professional positions in both small teams and large organizations.

BARBARA WELSS EVERSOLE, PhD, is an assistant professor in the Human Resource Development Program at Indiana State University. Her teaching areas are in strategic human resource development, program evaluation, and learner evaluation. Dr. Eversole's areas of research include work/life issues and executive coaching. She is the founder and senior consultant of Transformations Unlimited Associates, an organizational consulting firm specializing in executive, management, and organization development. Dr. Eversole has twenty years of experience in management, training and development, and coaching.